Exotic Gems

Volume 1

Above: An ensemble of tanzanite rings from Van Lachman. *Photo from Van Lachman.*

Opposite page: Oregon sunstone beads, earrings, pendant and loose sunstones from Rogue Gems LLC. The yellow oval is a Montana sapphire, the red trillion is a fire opal, and the large oval cab is a boulder opal. *Photo by Paul Quinn and Tino Hammid.*

Exotic Gems

Volume 1

How to Identify and Buy

Tanzanite, Ammolite, Rhodochrosite, Zultanite
Sunstone, Moonstone & Other Feldspars

Renée Newman

International Jewelry Publications
Los Angeles _____

A portion of the tanzanite section was first published in the *Emerald & Tanzanite Buying Guide* in 1996.

International Jewelry Publications
P.O. Box 13384
Los Angeles, CA 90013-0384 USA

(Inquiries should be accompanied by a self-addressed, stamped envelope.)

Printed in Singapore

Library of Congress Cataloging-in-Publication Data

Newman, Renée.
  Exotic Gems / Renée Newman.
    p. cm. – (Newman exotic gem series)
  Includes bibliographical references and index.
    ISBN-13: 978-0-929975-42-9 (trade pbk. : alk. paper)
1. Precious stones–Purchasing. 1. Title.
  TS752.N445 2010
  553.8--dc22
                                        2009037682

Front cover photos:
Ammolite Pendant and photo from Korite Internattional
Tanzanite Ring and photo from Erica Courtney™.
Oligoclase cut and photographed by John Dyer.
Rhodochrosite earring and photo from Timeless Gems
Oregon Sunstone carving and photo from Daylan Hargrave.
Zultanite and photo from Zultanite Gems LLC.
Rainbow moonstone from Northern India courtesy Boston Gems.
Photo by Robert & Orasa Weldon.

Contents

Acknowledgments

I would like to express my appreciation to the following people for their contribution to *Exotic Gems, Volume 1*:

Ernie and Regina Goldberger of the Josam Diamond Trading Corporation. This book could never have been written without the experience and knowledge I gained from working with them.

Mineralogist John S. White. He has edited a major portion of *Exotic Gems*. His recommendations and corrections have greatly improved this book.

American Gemological Laboratories (AGL), Canadian Institute of Gemmology, Gemmological Association of All Japan (GAAJ) Zenhokyo Lab, Gemological Institute of America (GIA), and Swiss Foundation for the Research of Gemstones (SSEF). They've contributed information, diagrams and/or photos.

Jillian Beck, Paul Cory, Gabriella Endlin, Jim Fiebig, Pete and Bobbi Flusser, Carrie Ginsberg, Alan Hodgkinson, Yoshi Kirsch, Dr. Horst Krupp, Wolf Kuehn, Bill Larson, Cynthia Marcusson, Linda McMurray, Marian Newton, Pierre Pare, Debra Sawatzky, Frank Schaffer, Nancy Schuring, Chris Smith, Abe Suleman, Ossi Treutler, Jr., Ev Tucker, John S. White, and John Woodmark. They've made valuable suggestions, corrections and comments regarding the portions of this book they examined. They are not responsible for any possible errors, nor do they necessarily endorse the material contained in this book.

Les Gemmes d'Orient, Inc., Carrie Ginsberg Fine Gems, Hubert Inc., Iteco, Inc., Jewels by Woods, Michael Kazanjian, New Era Gems, Overland Gems, Inc., Temple Trading Co, and Timeless Gems. Their stones or jewelry have been used for some of the photographs.

American Gemological Laboratories, Best Cut Gems, Boston Gems & Findings Inc., Martha Borzoni, Canadian Institute of Gemmology, I. M. Chait Gallery / Auctioneers, Classic Colors Inc., Cynthia Renée Co., Dancing Designs, David Clay Company, Erica Courtney, Paula Crevoshay, Tom DeGasperis, Desert Sun Mining & Gems, Devon Fine Jewelry, Different Seasons Jewelry, Mia Dixon, Jessica Dow, John and Lydia Dyer, FGS Gems, Freya's Jewellery, Henry Hänni, Daylan Hargrave, John & Margit Haupt, Alan Hodgkinson, Hubert Inc., Richard Hughes, Iteco Inc.,

Jewels by Woods, John Koivula, Korite International, Stephen Kotlowski, Dr. Horst Krupp, Wimon Manorotkul, Nevada Mineral & Book Co. New Era Gems, Pala International, Pearce Design, Rare Multicolor Gems, Cynthia Renée Co., Mark Schneider Design, Sherris Cottier Shank, Chris Smith, Tanzanite Foundation, Timeless Gems, Harold & Erica Van Pelt, Victor Velyan, Robert and Orasa Weldon, Larry Woods, Philip Zahm Designs, Zaffiro Clay Zava, and Zultanite, Inc. Photos or diagrams from them have been reproduced in this book.

Frank Chen and Joyce Ng. They provided technical assistance.

Louise Harris Berlin, editor of *Exotic Gems*. Thanks to her, this book is easier to read and understand.

My sincere thanks to all of these contributors for their kindness and help.

1

Exotic Gems

The term "exotic" has two definitions that apply to the gems in this book. According to the Merriam Webster Dictionary, "exotic" can refer to people, places or things that are:

1. of foreign origin or character; introduced from abroad

2. strikingly, excitingly or mysteriously different or unusual

To Canadian residents, ammolite is not foreign, but it comes from remote areas of Alberta and is strikingly unusual, so even to Canadians, ammolite is an exotic gem. From the perspective of Asians, Africans and South Americans, ammolite is definitely a foreign exotic gem.

Much has been written about diamonds, pearls, rubies, sapphires, opals and emeralds, but other gems are usually grouped together in general gem books such as my *Gemstone Buying Guide*, with limited information on each stone. Since readers have requested additional information on the less common types, I've decided to create a series of books entitled *Exotic Gems*, which will explore each gem more in depth. Besides ammolite, this first volume will include tanzanite, zultanite, rhodochrosite, and members of the feldspar family—labradorite, sunstone, moonstone, andesine, orthoclase, amazonite, and oligoclase.

Another motive for completing this volume is that several people have requested I write another book on tanzanite. In 1996, I came out with the first book on tanzanite, entitled *The Emerald & Tanzanite Buying Guide*. After the book sold out, the emerald portion was added to my *Ruby & Sapphire Buying Guide*. Some of the tanzanite information in that book, is included in this first volume of *Exotic Gems*. New photos and updated information on tanzanite have been added.

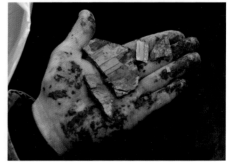

Fig. 1.1 Ammolite & photo from Korite Intl.

Fig. 1.2 The snows of Kilimanjaro rise in majestic splendor from Merelani's tanzanite mines. This ice-capped dormant volcano is not just Africa's highest peak, but at 5,895 meters (19,340 ft), also one of the world's tallest freestanding mountains. *Photo © Richard W. Hughes.*

Fig. 1.3 Miners extracting tanzanite. *Photo © Tanzanite Foundation.*

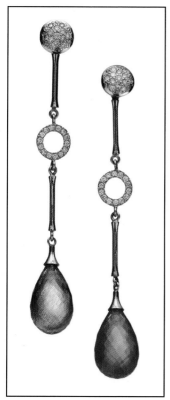

Fig. 1.4 Oregon sunstone earrings from Rogue Gems, LLC. *Photo: Robert & Orasa Weldon.*

Fig. 1.5 Banks of the St. Mary River in Southern Alberta Canada, where most of the commercial mining of ammolite has been conducted. *Photo from Korite Internaional.*

Fig. 1.6 Digging for Oregon sunstone in the desert. *Photo from Rogue Gems, LLC.*

Fig. 1.6 Inspecting veins of zultanite in a mine in Turkey. *Photo from Zultanite Gems LLC.*

Fig. 1.7 Admiring a zultanite crystal. *Photo from Zultanite Gems LLC.*

My gem guides typically contain more information on gemstone evaluation than those by other authors. This book is no exception. The next chapter provides a general overview of gemstone price factors using examples of the gems discussed in this book. Additional evaluation information is given in the chapters on the individual gems.

It's important for you to learn how to judge the quality of gems so that you'll have a greater appreciation for their uniqueness. A great deal of time and skill is required to bring out their beauty. Though nature provides us with the raw material for exotic stones, man is largely responsible for their brilliance and sparkle. If you have a good understanding of the factors that affect gem value, this will help you make wise selections that you'll enjoy for a lifetime.

The third chapter focuses on treatments used to improve the color and clarity of the gems in this book. The treatment status of a gem can be an important price factor. Gems of natural color and clarity are normally more valuable than treated gems. However, in some cases, treatments may not affect the price if they are routinely done and well accepted. The heat treatment of tanzanite is an example. On the other hand, coating tanzanite to improve its color is not an accepted trade practice.

Chapter 4 will help you understand the identification tables throughout the book. It explains terminology that gemologists use to describe the optical, physical and chemical properties of gems. Basic gem identification tips will be given in the subsequent chapters along with identification data in order to help you detect imitations. You'll also learn about the history, lore, geographic sources and proper care of the gems discussed in this book.

Numerous photos are provided to illustrate quality evaluation, mining, gem types, jewelry styles, and the gemological concepts discussed in this book. I've taken some of the photos, but many dealers, jewelers, designers, and gem labs have also contributed images. Even though photos can't accurately reproduce color, they give you a general idea of the wide variety of colors of the gems discussed in this volume. As you learn to examine their color nuances, you'll see why gems like these have been prized for so long. As the eminent gemologist George Frederick Kunz has pointed out, their colors have an unusual enduring quality:

"All the fair colors of flowers and foliage, and even the blue of the sky and the glory of the sunset clouds, only last a short time, and are subject to continual change, but the sheen and coloration of precious stones are the same today as they were thousands of years ago and will be for thousands of years to come. In a world of change, this permanence has a charm of its own that was early appreciated." (*The Curious Lore of Precious Stones*, preface, page XV.)

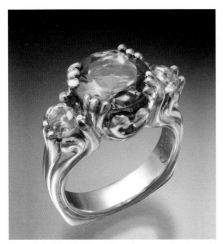

Fig. 2.1 The light-colored tanzanite in this ring by Pearce Design flatters women who look good in pastel colors, but costs less than deep blue tanzanite. *Photo: Ralph Gabriner.*

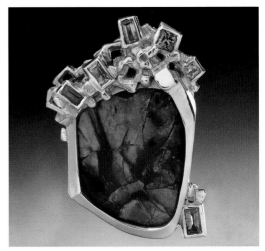

Fig. 2.2 Ammolite pendant by Fred & Kate Pearce featuring autumn colors. *Photo by Ralph Gabriner.*

Fig. 2.3 A deep blue tanzanite. *Photo and ring from Hubert Inc.*

Fig. 2.4 Each of these pink tanzanites cut by Clay Zava is attractive, but the one with the stronger pink color is more valued. *Photo by Robert Weldon.*

Fig. 2.5 Oregon sunstone with a highly valued red color from Desert Sun Mining & Gems. *Photo by Daniel Van Rossen.*

Fig. 2.6 These lighter colored Oregon sunstones from Desert Sun Mining & Gems are more affordable than the one in fig 2.5. *Photo: Dan Van Rossen.*

Price Factors in a Nutshell

The following factors can affect the prices of tanzanite, zultanite, ammolite, rhodochrosite, sunstone, moonstone, and other feldspars.

♦ **Color**

♦ **Clarity** (degree to which a stone is free from flaws)

♦ **Cutting style & shape**

♦ **Cut quality** (proportions and finish)

♦ **Carat weight or stone size**

♦ **Transparency**

♦ **Treatment status** (untreated or treated? type and extent of treatment)

♦ **Brilliance**

♦ **Brand name or designer's trademark**

♦ **Presence and distinctness of phenomena** (e.g., cat's-eye, iridescence)

Price Factors Explained

COLOR plays a major role in gem pricing, but its impact varies depending on the quality, size, variety and species of a gemstone. (A variety is a category within a gem species; e.g., tanzanite is a variety of zoisite, which is a species.) Color has a greater effect on the price of tanzanite, for example, than on most rhodochrosite. Here are some guidelines:

In most cases, the stronger and more saturated the color, the more it is valued. For example, a strong blue tanzanite (fig. 2.3) can cost many times more than a pale blue tanzanite all other factors being equal.

Some people prefer medium blue tanzanites to those with a deep blue color and for them, the lighter color is a better choice. Lavender and light blue tanzanites can flatter people who look good in pastel colors (fig. 2.1).

In most cases, the more grayish, brownish or blackish a gemstone is, the lower its price, unless it's supposed to be black or brown. Buyers normally prefer stones with good color saturation; nevertheless, just because a stone is brownish or black, does not mean it's undesirable. Consider the ammolite pendant in figure 2.2. Many people would reject a stone with brown areas like those on this ammolite. Yet this piece would be attractive on anybody who looks good in autumn colors..

The more rare a color is, the more it may be valued, if there is a demand for the color. Red and green are the rarest colors for Oregon sunstone, so they are the most highly valued. In ammolite, blue is more rare so it's more prized. It's the rarity of the color, rather than color itself, that often determines prices.

In most cases, the lower the quality of a stone, the less impact color has on price. Color has little influence on the price of low-grade translucent to opaque stones, but it has a significant effect on top-grade gems.

Low price does not necessarily mean low desirability. Light colored, low-priced gems can be quite attractive when well cut. To learn more on how color affects the price of different gem varieties, see Chapters 5–12.

CLARITY is the degree to which a gemstone is free from external marks called **blemishes** and internal features called **inclusions**. Sometimes the jewelry trade refers to them as **clarity characteristics** or **identifying features**. **Flaw** is a term that is sometimes used in this book because it's short and clear. It refers to both blemishes and inclusions. Usually, the fewer, smaller and less noticeable the flaws, the higher the price, especially for higher priced gems. However, there tends to be a greater tolerance for flaws in colored gems than in diamonds. One exception is tanzanite, which is normally eye-clean (free of flaws visible to the unaided eye) and often loupe clean (free of flaws visible with a 10-power loupe).

Even though terms like "flaw" and "blemish" have negative connotations, their presence can be positive. Flaws are identifying marks that can help you identify your stone at any time. They can lower the price of a gemstone without affecting its beauty. Flaws are especially important evidence that your stone is natural.

Opinions differ as to how various clarity features should be classified. Some think the term "inclusion" should be reserved for foreign matter within a gemstone. This book uses a broader definition, which is found in the *GIA Diamond Grading Course*: "**Inclusions** are characteristics which are entirely inside a stone or extend into it from the surface." The GIA defines **blemishes** as "characteristics confined to or primarily affecting the surface." ons differ as to how various clarity features should be classified.

Listed below are inclusions found in tanzanite, rhodochrosite, zultanite, sunstone, moonstone and other feldspars.

♦ **Crystals** (fig. 2.7 & 2.12) are solid mineral inclusions of various shapes and sizes. Minute crystals are sometimes called **pinpoints** or **grains,** and when they are grouped together, they are called **clouds.**

♦ **Needles** are long, thin inclusions that are either solid crystals or tubes filled with gas or liquid, which are called **growth tubes** (figs. 2.9 & 2.11).

Fig. 2.7 Ruby crystals in feldspar. *Photo © John I. Koivula.*

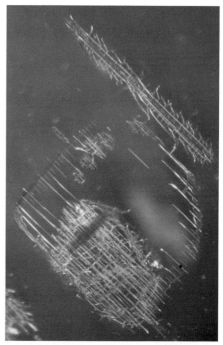

Fig. 2.8 "Centipede" inclusions in orthoclase moonstone. *Photo © John I. Koivula.*

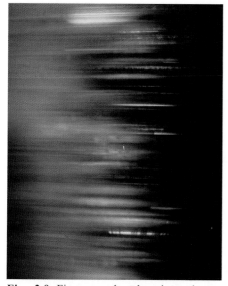

Fig. 2.9 Fine growth tubes in cat's-eye tanzanite. *Photo © John I. Koivula.*

Fig. 2.10 Lamellar twinning in labradorite from Oregon. *Photo © John I. Koivula.*

The above photos are from the *Photoatlas of Inclusions in Gemstones, Volume 2*, by Eduard Gübelin and John Koivula. For more info, go to www.john-koivula.microworldofgems.com.

◆ **Cracks** (also called **fractures** or **fissures)** of various sizes are common inclusions (figs. 2.13 & 2.14). Because of their appearance, cracks are often referred to in the trade as **feathers**. Grouping of tiny fractures resembling centipedes is a characteristic of moonstone (fig. 2.8).

◆ **Parting (false cleavage)**, which occurs in feldspar, refers to breakage along a plane of weakness.

◆ **Twinning** can occur when two or more crystals of the same mineral are united with a symmetric relationship. In feldspar, twinning may appear as straight lines, which are in essence flattened twinning planes, or they may look like rows or boards. This tabular-like twinning is called **lamellar twinning** (fig. 2.10).

◆ **Fingerprints** are thought to be healed cracks. These inclusions often look like human fingerprints, but they may also resemble wispy veils.

◆ **Growth or color zoning** refers to an uneven distribution of color in a stone. If the different color zones look like bands, they're called **growth or color bands.** Color zoning is especially common in Oregon sunstone.

◆ **Cavities** are holes or indentations extending into a stone from the surface. Cavities can result when negative crystals or tubes are exposed or when solid crystals are pulled out of a stone during the cutting process.

There is no universally accepted grading system for colored gems. My *Ruby, Sapphire & Emerald Buying Guide* discusses three grading systems that are used by gemologists. When buying stones, you don't have to be able to assign a grade to it. However, it is helpful to know how to determine if the inclusions detract from its beauty or threaten its durability.

You should judge the clarity of colored stones using overhead lighting both with and without magnification. A loupe (hand magnifier) or a microscope can help you see potentially damaging flaws that might escape the unaided eye. Overhead lighting is above the stone, not literally over a person's head. The light is reflected from the facets of a gem back to the viewer's eye. Overhead illumination is a natural way of lighting which does not exaggerate flaws or hide brilliance. It therefore helps you make a fair assessment of a gemstone's appearance.

When professionals use microscopes to judge clarity, they usually examine the stones with a type of lighting called **darkfield illumination—** back lighting with a dark background, in which diffused light comes up diagonally through the bottom of the gemstone. In other words, the diffused light is transmitted through the stone, instead of being reflected back to the eye. (A frosted or shaded bulb provides diffused light. A clear bulb does not.) With darkfield illumination, tiny inclusions and even dust particles will stand out in high relief. As a result, the clarity of the stone appears worse than it would under normal conditions.

Fig. 2.11 Needle inclusions in tanzanite. *Photo by author.*

Fig. 2.12 A crystal, fingerprint and pinpoint inclusions in tanzanite. *Photo by author.*

Fig. 2.13 A tanzanite in overhead light. In terms of appearance, the clarity is not bad, but the central crack is a durability threat, especially since tanzanite cleaves easily. *Photo by author.*

Fig. 2.14 Darkfield illumination turns a hardly noticeable "fingerpirnt" into a distracting inclusion. Ten-power magnification through a microscope was used for this stone. *Photo by author.*

Since darkfield illumination highlights details of inclusions, it's useful for detecting synthetics, imitations, treatments and place of origin. Darkfield illumination can help determine the depth of cracks, the type of filling present in fractures, and the extent to which a stone has been treated.

Even if you are able to use darkfield illumination as an assessment tool, be sure to use overhead lighting in your final evaluation of a gem's beauty because it provides the most realistic view of the stone. Dealers use overhead lighting when pricing gems. They typically examine stones under a fluorescent lamp with and without a loupe (usually 10-power).

Grades are helpful for documentation purposes, but you don't need them to judge clarity and transparency. Look at the rhodochrosites in figure 2.15. It's obvious from their appearance that they are arranged in the order of their decreasing clarity and that the stone at the far left has the best clarity.

Judging Clarity

Fig. 2.15 These rhodochrosites are arranged in the order of their decreasing clarity. The stone at the far left has the best clarity. *Gemstones from Iteco, Inc; photo by author.*

Fig. 2.17 *Photo by author.*

Fig. 2.16 *Photo by author.*

Fig. 2.18 *Photo by author.*

Look at the tanzanites in figures 2.16 to 2.18. Which do you think has the best clarity and which has the worst? If you chose figure 2.16 as the best and figure 2.18 as the worst, then you have just proved to yourself that you can make a clarity judgment without the aid of grades.

Incidentally, tanzanite dealers wouldn't consider the stone in figure 2.18 suitable for jewelry use, and many would not mount the tanzanite in figure 2.17. The clarity of tanzanites is usually better than that of many diamonds. For the most part, jewelry-quality tanzanites are at least eye-clean. Rhodochrosites on the other hand tend to be more included than diamonds and tanzanites.

TRANSPARENCY is the degree to which light passes through a material so that objects are visible through it. In other words, it's the degree to which a gem is clear, hazy, translucent or opaque. Transparency and clarity are interlinked because flaws can block the passage of light. Gemologists use the following terms to describe gem transparency.

◆ **Transparent**—objects seen through the gemstone look clear and distinct.

◆ **Semitransparent**—objects look slightly hazy or blurry through the stone.

◆ **Translucent**—objects are vague and hard to see. Imagine reading print through frosted glass—that is translucency.

◆ **Semitranslucent**—In this book, I use it to mean partially translucent and partially opaque. Other gemologists may use the term as a synonym of semi-opaque, which in my opinion, denotes a lower transparency.

◆ **Semiopaque**—only a small fraction of light passes through the stone, mainly around the edges.

◆ **Opaque**—virtually no light can pass through the gemstone.

Dealers often use other terms to designate the transparency of a gem, some of which are:

◆ crystal (highly transparent)   ◆ sleepy
◆ highly transparent   ◆ looks like soap
◆ milky   ◆ looks like jade
◆ cloudy   ◆ has poor (or low) transparency

Transparency can have a major impact on the value of a gemstone, especially for sunstone, rhodochrosite and zoisite. Normally the higher the transparency, the more valuable the stone, although there are a few exceptions. For example, moonstones with microscopic particles which disperse a blue color and increase their adularescence (glowing effect) are normally more valued than moonstones with high transparency.

SHAPE is a gem's face-up outline (e.g., round or pear shaped).The effect of shape on price varies depending on the seller, the gem variety, the stone weight, the stone quality and the demand for the shape. The subject of shape pricing is complex. Simply remember to compare gemstones of the same shape and cutting style when evaluating gem prices.

Transparency Examples

Fig. 2.19 The transparent rhodochrosite on the left costs more than the semitransparent rhodochrosite on the right even though they're about the same size, shape and color. Transparency is an important value factor. *Stones from Iteco Inc; photo by author.*

Fig. 2.20 Translucent rhodochrosite. *Earring & photo from Timeless Gems.*

Fig. 2.21 Semitranslucent rhodochrosite. (Partially translucent, partially opaque). *Photo by author.*

Fig. 2.22 Transparent pink zoisite (pink tanzanite) cut by Clay Zava from David Clay Co. *Photo by Robert Weldon.*

Fig. 2.23 Translucent to opaque pink zoisite (thulite). Most thulite is semiopaque. Past 6mm thickness, no light is transmitted. *Rough and pendant from Nevada Mineral & Book Co. Photo by Sandy and Walter Lombardo.*

The symmetry of the shape outline can also affect the per-carat price of large, high quality gems because symmetrical stones are desirable and may require more loss of weight from the rough.

Gemstone Terms Defined

Before you can thoroughly understand a discussion of cutting styles, it's helpful to learn some basic terminology. These terms are illustrated in figure 2.24 and explained below:

Facets: The polished surfaces or planes on a stone. Normally they are flat, but some cutters are now creating stones with concave facets. Facets are intended to create brilliance in a gemstone.

Table: The large, flat top facet. It normally has an octagonal shape on a round stone.

Girdle: The narrow rim around the stone. The girdle plane is parallel to the table and is the largest diameter of any part of the stone.

Crown: The upper part of the stone above the girdle.

Pavilion: The lower part of the stone below the girdle.

Culet: The tiny facet on the pointed bottom of the pavilion, parallel to the table. Sometimes the point of a

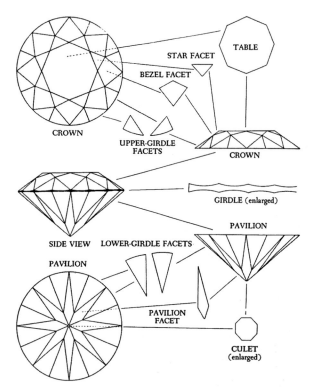

Fig. 2.24 Basic terminology and facet arrangement of a standard round brilliant cut. *Reprinted with permission from the Gemological Institute of America.*

stone is called "the culet" even if no culet facet is present, which is usually the case with rubies and sapphires.

Fancy Shape: For colored stones, it is any shape except round and square. For diamonds, "fancy shape" refers to all shapes except round.

Rough: Gem material in its natural state as it comes out of the ground prior to cutting or polishing.

Gemstone Shapes

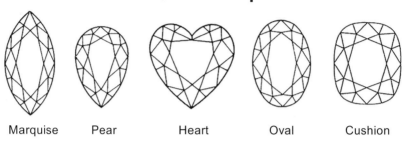

Marquise   Pear   Heart   Oval   Cushion

Fig. 2.25 Modified triangle, modified pear, or modified shield. Tanzanite from Carrie Ginsberg Fine Gems. *Photo by author.*

Fig. 2.26 Emerald-cut triangle. *Zultanite from Zultanite Gems LLC.*

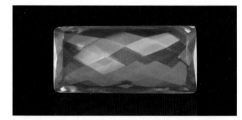

Fig. 2.27 Rectangular moonstone from Boston Gems. *Photo by Robert and Orasa Weldon.*

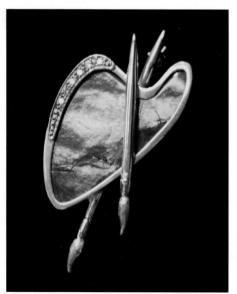

Fig. 2.28 Freeform ammolite pendant from Freya's Jewellery. *Photo by Ossi Treutler Jr.*

Fig. 2.29 Calf's-head. *Oregon sunstone from Rogue Gems LLC. Photo: Robert & Orasa Weldon.*

Gemstone Cutting Styles

Gemstones can be either faceted or unfaceted like the tanzanite cabochon in figure 2.29. There are three basic styles:

Step cut: Has rows of facets that resemble the steps of a staircase. The facets are usually four-sided and elongated, and parallel to the girdle. Emerald cuts are step cuts with clipped corners.

Brilliant cut: Has rows of facets that resemble the steps of a staircase. The facets are usually four-sided and elongated, and parallel to the girdle

Mixed cut: Has both styles of faceting.

Fig. 2.29 Tanzanite oval cabochon. *Ring and photo from I. M. Chait Gallery / Auctioneers.*

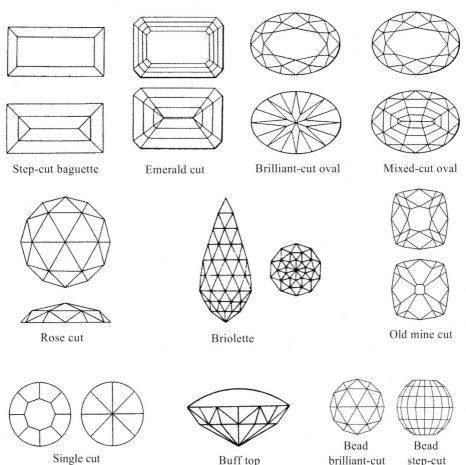

Step-cut baguette   Emerald cut   Brilliant-cut oval   Mixed-cut oval

Rose cut   Briolette   Old mine cut

Single cut   Buff top   Bead brilliant-cut   Bead step-cut

CUTTING STYLE is the way in which a stone is cut or faceted. **Cabochon**s (unfaceted dome-shaped stones) and unfaceted beads are generally priced lower than faceted stones because they cost less to cut than faceted styles.

Another reason cabochons are usually priced less is that they're often made from lower quality material that is unsuitable for faceting. One exception is moonstone. The finest moonstone material is usually reserved for cabs because they display so well the stone's characteristic shifting glow. Cabochons stones of other gem varieties can also be of high quality, especially those found in antique jewelry.

Designer and trademarked cutting styles often sell for more than generic cuts of the same shape. The more complex the cutting style and the more renowned the cutter, the higher the price may be.

CUT QUALITY refers to the proportions and finish, also called **make**. This is a crucial factor because it affects the brilliance and color of gems, but its importance is not always reflected in the price of colored gems. Two of the main considerations of cut quality are:

1. **Do you see color all across the stone when you look at it face up?** Well-cut stones don't have large black areas nor do they have an obvious **window**—a pale, washed out area in the middle of stones that allows you to see right through them. In general, the larger the window, the poorer the cut. An even color throughout the stone indicates good cut quality.

2. **Are you paying for excess weight?** Suppose you have two stones with the same face-up size that are priced by carat weight. One is well cut and one has an overly deep and fat bottom and weighs twice as much if it had the same per-carat price. The overly deep stone would cost twice as much even though it has the same face-up size. In addition, it may be impractical for mounting and appear overly dark. Keep in mind, however, that colored gems with good brilliance and color must often be cut deeper than diamonds. If colored stones are cut too shallow, they will have a window.

BRILLIANCE generally refers to the brightness of a gem, which is the actual and/or perceived amount of light returned by the stone. Sometimes brilliance can have a broader meaning. For example, in her book *Diamond Grading ABC,* Pagel-Theisen states that the term "brilliance" involves several distinct optical processes in a diamond— internal brilliance, external brilliance (luster), dispersive brilliance (fire), and scintillation brilliance (sparkle) (pp 176-177). The American Gem Society defines brilliance as "brightness plus positive contrast." In other words, besides appearing bright, a brilliant stone has an attractive distribution of contrasting dark and bright areas.

Judging Cut Quality

Fig. 2.30 Tanzanite with a "window" allowing you to see through the stone. *Photo by author.*

Fig. 2.31 An exceptional tanzanite cut by John Dyer. *Photo by Lydia Dyer.*

Fig. 2.32 Profile view of a well proportioned tanzanite from Overland Gems. *Photo by author.*

Fig. 2.33 Face-up view of the tanzanite in figure 2.32. No windowing is present. *Photo by author.*

Fig. 2.34 Tanzanite with a shallow pavilion and thick girdle. Stones cut like this have a window face up. *Photo by author.*

Fig. 2.35 Sunstone with a large window. *Photo by Wolf Kuehn of the Canadian Inst. of Gemmology.*

Judging Brilliance

Fig. 2.36 Oregon sunstones with varying degrees of brilliance from Desert Sun Mining and Gems. *Photo by Daniel Van Rossen.*

Fig. 2.37 Ammolite with low brilliance. *Stone & photo: Korite International.*

Fig. 2.39 Ammolite with good brilliance. *Stone and photo from Korite International.*

Fig. 2.40 Ammolite with average brilliance. *Stone and photo from Korite International.*

Fig. 2.42 The same labradorite looks dull and dark from a different angle. *Photo by author.*

Fig. 2.41 Labradorite with good brilliance when viewed from the proper angle. *Photo by author.*

CARAT WEIGHT OR STONE SIZE is also an important value factor. In most cases, the higher the carat-weight category, the greater the per-carat price of a gem. A carat is a unit of weight equaling 1/5 of a gram.

Many translucent to opaque stones are sold by the piece or stone size, not by weight. Designer cuts may also be priced per piece, and colored stones under approximately half a carat are often priced according to millimeter size.

TREATMENT STATUS includes three elements which can be important if you're spending a substantial amount of money on a gemstone:

1. **Is the stone treated or untreated?** Has the stone undergone a process other than cleaning, cutting or polishing to improve its natural appearance? Most colored stones are treated in some way by man. High quality untreated gems are usually the most highly valued because they're more rare and they're natural. However, an ugly untreated stone is typically worth less and harder to sell than one that is attractive and treated. That's why gems are treated.

2. **What tr eatment(s) did the stone undergo?** Not all treatments are equal. Some treatments, such as dyeing and coating have a more negative impact on value than others, like heat treatment, which is well accepted. Therefore it pays to find out which gem treatments were used on a gem before assessing its value. The next chapter discusses the various types of gem treatments.

3. **What is the extent of treatment?** This applies to clarity enhancements such as fracture filling. A stone with a minor amount of filling is more valued than one with a substantial amount throughout the stone.

DISTINCTNESS OF PHENOMENA

Phenomena are unusual optical effects such as:

♦ **Chatoyancy** (cat's-eye): a band of reflected light in cabochons (gems with a domed, polished surface). It occurs when a strong light strikes needle-like inclusions or hollow tubes that are parallel within the stone. A cat's-eye effect may be seen occasionally on tanzanite and feldspar. Top quality cat's-eye stones have a sharp, straight, narrow band in the center of the cabochon. The band is distinct and not too thin. (Fig. 2.45)

♦ **Adularescence**: a floating, shifting, billowy light effect caused by structural unevenness in moonstone, which scatters the light. The brighter and more noticeable the adularescence, the better the moonstone. (Fig. 2.47)

♦ **Aventurescence**: a glittery, sparkling effect caused by light reflecting off tiny platelike inclusions. In sunstone, the inclusions are usually platelets of copper or hematite. (Fig. 2.48)

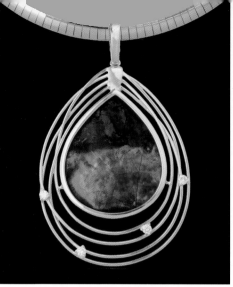

Fig. 2.43 Iridescence in ammolite. *Pendant and photo from Korite International.*

Fig. 2.44 Labradorescence and iridescence in a spectrolite cut by Gail O. Clark. *Cabochon from Different Seasons Jewelry; photo: Jessica Dow.*

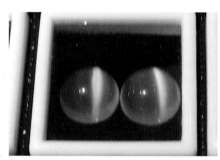

Fig. 2.45 Cat's-eye moonstone from Temple Trading Company. *Photo by author.*

Fig. 2.46 Labradorescence in labradorite. *Photo by author.*

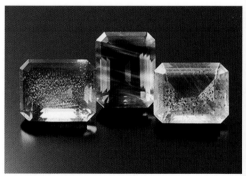

Fig. 2.47 Adularescence in moonstone. *Ring from Boston Gems; photo: Robert & Orasa Weldon.*

Fig. 2.48 Aventurescence (schiller) in Oregon sunstones from Desert Sun Mining and Gems. *Photo by Wayne Jones.*

Fig. 2.49 Color change in zultanite—pastel yellowish green in daylight to pale pink in low wattage incandescent light and candlelight. *Zultanites and photo from Zultanite Gems LLC.*

♦ **Color change:** sometimes called the alexandrite effect, it's a change of color that occurs when the light source is altered. For example, zultanite can change from pastel yellowish green in daylight equivalent lighting to a light gold under traditional light bulbs and to a muted purplish pink under candlelight or low wattage light bulbs. (Fig. 2.49)

♦ **Labradorescence:** a flash of color(s) in labradorite or spectrolite seen at certain viewing angles. It's caused by the interference of light through the layered structure of the labradorite. (Figs. 2.44 & 2.46)

♦ **Iridescence**: a play of lustrous changing colors caused by the interference of light. The GIA (Gemological Institute of America) uses it to refer to the color phenomena of gems such as ammolite, fire agate, and rainbow agate (figs. 2.43, 2.44, 2.46). The colors must have a shifting quality rather than a static, fixed position like you'll see in banded agate or watermelon tourmaline (color zoning).

"Iridescence" has different meanings to different trade members. Some feel that a gem must show all colors of the rainbow to be classified as iridescent; others require at least three colors, and still others would classify a solid red ammolite as iridescent as long as the quality of the color changes when the stone is moved. Many people extend the meaning of "iridescence" to describe the phenomena of gems such as opals and labradorite.

In general, the sharper and more obvious the phenomena, the more valuable the stone, all other factors being equal. However, don't expect the phenomena of natural stones to be as distinct as those on man-made stones. For example, the sharper and more noticeable a star, the more valuable the stone, unless it's a synthetic star. Natural stars are not as perfect as those on man-made stones.

Colored Gem Pricing

Some consumers think that dealers evaluate colored gems in a logical, analytical manner. Unlike diamond dealers, colored-gem dealers do not assign color and clarity grades according to a standardized grading system, nor do they list proportion measurements such as the angle of the top of the stone (crown angle).

Colored-gem dealers tend to evaluate gem quality as a whole rather than breaking it down to its constituent parts of color, clarity, transparency, proportions, etc. Their final judgments are usually more intuitive than logical. Non quality related factors also enter into their pricing strategies. Some of these price determinants are demand, form of payment, buyer's credit rating, amount purchased, competitors' prices. time of sale, the customer's eagerness to buy, the seller's need for money and his assessment of the buyer. Astute, knowledgeable buyers tend to be offered better prices.

Since you can't always count on prices to reflect the quality of gems, it's all the more important that you learn to make quality judgments yourself. The reason this book analyzes color and gem quality in terms of their component parts is to aid you in this process. Vague statements such as "look for color" are not helpful to consumers. However, when you learn how color elements and price factors affect the cost of a gem, it's easier for you to understand gem valuation. Your ultimate goal should be to feel confident making quick comprehensive judgments about gem quality, as a dealer would. But like any other skill, this takes practice.

Independent gem lab documents and appraisals are recommended for verifying the identity, origin and treatment status of expensive gemstones, especially for major purchases. Even experienced dealers realize the need for assistance from reputable gem labs when buying and selling gems. Consult the *Gem & Jewelry Pocket Guide* by Renée Newman for sample lab documents. Information on selecting appraisers is provided in Chapter 13 and on my website www.reneenewman.com. Click on the appraisers tab.

For most gems, the price ranges are broad because of the variability in the quality. You can find very low-grade sunstones at public gem shows retailing for as low as $10. On the other hand, you can find large top-grade sunstones retailing for as much as $10,000.

Use the price ranges in this book only as a general guideline of the relative values of gems. They may be obsolete when you read them, so do your own comparison shopping, and deal with knowledgeable sellers who will look after your interests. Don't become so focused on price that you overlook aesthetic features. Gems do not have to be top quality to be acceptable, but they should meet *your* needs in terms of beauty and pizazz.

Gem Treatments

In this book, the term **"treatment"** refers to any human-controlled process other than cutting or polishing that alters the original appearance of a gem, e.g., heating, fracture filling, dyeing, etc. The term **"enhancement"** is used by the trade as an alternative word for treatment, especially when making disclosures in advertisements and on lab reports. However, treatments don't always enhance a gemstone's appearance or its value.

CIBJO (the French acronym for The World Jewelry Confederation) uses the term **modification** to refer to gem treatments. CIBJO divides modified gemstones into two classes: one that requires general information of their modification (e.g., heating) and one that requires specific information (e.g., diffusion treatment and dyeing).

Most tanzanites and ammolites are treated. Rhodochroisite, zultanite, and most feldspars, however, are normally not treated. Two exceptions are amazonite and andesine. This chapter describes only the treatments that are applied to the gems discussed in this book.

HEAT TREATMENT: Many gems such as tanzanite are heated to improve their color. Unlike sapphire, which is often heated at temperature above 1600°C (2900°F), tanzanite is slowly heated to 400-650°C. This process turns tanzanite that is brown into an attractive blue to purple color. The color is stable. Heat-treated tanzanite is usually priced the same as unheated tanzanite of the same color.

IRRADIATION: This is a process by which a gem is exposed to radiation. Various types of radiation are used to intensify or change the color of certain gems. Gamma rays from a cobalt or cesium source are the preferred irradiation agent because they don't induce radioactivity. On rare occasions, white microcline is irradiated to turn it into blue amazonite.

FRACTURE & CAVITY FILLING: If surface fractures in gems are filled with an appropriate substance, the fractures are less noticeable and the overall color and transparency may improve. Oil, wax, glass, resins or polymers are used as fillers. Some fillings can evaporate over time and leave a white or brown residue. Cavities and fractures in ammolite are filled with polymers or lacquer during a stabilization process. Any stone with surface reaching fractures can be fracture-filled, but dealers who want to market their gems as completely natural do not fracture-fill their stones. Most fillers are affected by the heat of a jeweler's torch.

DIFFUSION OF FOREIGN COLORING ELEMENTS: When heating drives elements such as copper, titanium or beryllium into certain gems, various colorations can result. For example, when copper is diffused into pale yellow andesine during heat treatment, red and green colors can be produced. As of the publication date of this book, gem labs are unable to positively determine whether an andesine is untreated or not. As a result, smart sellers are now identifying their red and green andesine as diffusion treated until they can prove otherwise.

COATING: Coating gems with a colored substance is an old technique, but recent advancements to the technology have caused a resurgence of coatings in the commercial market. In May 2008, the American Gem Trade Association Gem Testing Center (AGTA GTC) and the American Gemological Laboratories (AGL) announced that they'd received tanzanites that had been coated on their pavilion (bottom side). They ranged in size from 0.29–4.22 carats. The small stones were immediately suspect because of their great depth of color, which is uncommon for uncoated tanzanites in these sizes. However, the coating on the larger stones was not immediately evident. Magnification was required to detect the treatment. Immersion in solutions such as alcohol or even water were also helpful.

Under magnification and reflected light, coated tanzanites may display abraded areas, gaps and surface iridescence (fig. 3.3). It's also helpful to examine the stones when immersed in liquid (fig. 3.5). Be suspicious when small stones have an unusually strong color. Unlike sapphire, deep blue tanzanites are not normally available in small sizes.

Fig 3.1 Sapphires were used as accents for this ring because it wasn't possible to find small tanzanites with the same depth of color as the center tanzanite. Be suspicious of small deep blue tanzanites. They may be coated. *Ring and photo from Hubert Inc.*

Moonstones and ammolites (in triplets) are occasionally coated with a black or colored substance to enhance color and/or adularescence.

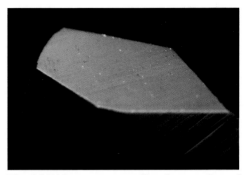

Fig. 3.3 Iridescence on pavilion facet surface of coated stone in reflected light. *Photo by* Makoto Okano / *GAAJ-Zenhokyo Laboratory.*

Fig. 3.2 Coated zoisite (tanzanite). *Photo from GAAJ-Zenhokyo Laboratory*

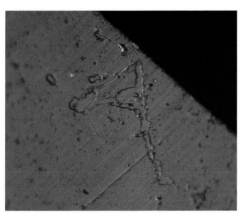

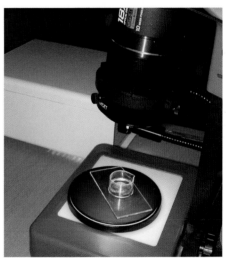

Fig. 3.4 Pits, scratches, and particles seen on the coating when viewed in reflected light. *Photo by Dr.Jun Kawano GAAJ Zenhokyo Laboratory.*

Fig. 3.5 Immersion cell used when examining stones for treatments such as coating and diffusion of foreign elements. *Photo by Wolf Kuehn of the Canadian Inst. of Gemmology.*

IMPREGNATION WITH WAX OR COLORLESS POLYMERS: Gems are waxed and plasticized to hide cracks and to make the surface look shiny. Impregnation can also improve durability and color. Ammolite is normally impregnated with a polymer to make it more durable. Amazonite is commonly waxed.

DYEING: Stones that have small surface cracks are sometimes dyed with colored oils, epoxies or dyes, especially if they're of low quality. However, the gems discussed in this book are normally not dyed.

Even though gem treatments are supposed to be disclosed, it's wise to ask sellers if their stones are treated. If they say they're untreated, ask them to write that on the receipt. It's best to have major purchases checked by a gem lab. Treatments are becoming more sophisticated and harder to detect.

Gem Identification Terminology

The previous two chapters provided basic information on gem treatments and quality evaluation. This chapter explains terminology used in the gem identification sections of this book.

Gemstones may be identified as a group, species, variety, or series member. A **group** is composed of a number of closely related species. "Feldspar" is an example of a group name. A **species** name refers to a mineral with a characteristic crystal structure and chemical composition. Microcline is one of the species of the feldspar group. A **variety** name is normally based on color, transparency or optical effects such as iridescence and cat's-eye patterns. For example, amazonite is a green variety of microcline; tanzanite and thulite are varieties of zoisite. They have the same essential chemistry and crystal structure but differ in color and/or transparency.

Groups may also have a subcategory called a **series**, which has members of variable chemical composition. For example, with feldspar there is the plagioclase series with members that contain varying proportions of calcium to sodium (andesine and labradorite are examples).

Trade names or **commercial names** are often given to gemstones by dealers to help promote their stones. "Spectrolite" is a trade name given to a colorful labradorite from Finland. Over time, trade names may gradually gain official status as variety names. For example, "tanzanite" was introduced in 1968 as a trade name for blue to violet zoisite. Now many gemologists identify it as tanzanite on their reports and classify it as a variety of zoisite. However, as of the publication date of this book, the World Jewellery Confederation labels "tanzanite" as an accepted commercial name, unlike sapphire which the organization designates as both a variety and commercial name for sapphire. On the other hand, the ICA (International Colored Gemstone Association) defines "tanzanite" as a blue variety of zoisite.

Some names such as moonstone and sunstone have become **popular names**. They are old terms that have evolved over time to describe gems with certain optical characteristics. Sunstone and moonstone are also considered to be commercial names.

Fig. 4.1 Refractometer, an instrument used to measure the refractive index of a gem. *Photo by Wolf Kuehn / Canadian Inst. of Gemmology.*

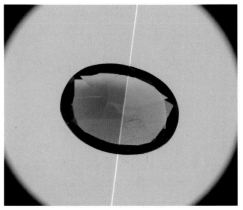

Fig. 4.2 Pleochroism of Oregon sunstone seen through a dichroscope. *Photo by Wolf Kuehn of the Canadian Inst. of Gemmology.*

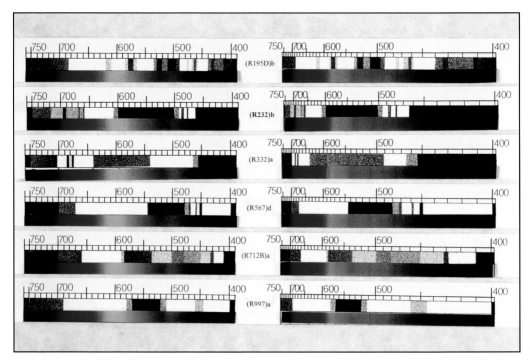

Fig. 4.3 The six spectra on the left illustrate the absorption patterns for six red stones seen through a diffraction-grating spectroscope. To the right are the spectra of the same stones as seen through a prism spectroscope. From the top the spectrum identities are almandine garnet, ruby, red spinel, red tourmaline, red beryl and glass. *Photo and spectra drawings by Alan Hodgkinson.*

Misnomers are names which do not correctly identify a gem. "Colorado Jade" and "Pikes Peak Jade" are misnomers for amazonite.

Each gem species or series member has characteristics which distinguish it from other species or series members. For easy reference, we'll list some of these characteristics below with their definitions.

Refractive Index (RI): the degree to which light is bent as it passes through the stone. This is measured with an instrument called a refractometer (fig. 4.1). Most colored gems have RI's that range between 1.43 and 1.98. Diamonds have an RI of approximately 2.42, which means they bend light about 2.42 times more than air does. This also means that light travels 2.42 times more slowly through diamonds than it does through air. As a general rule, the higher the RI is, the greater the potential brilliance of the stone. Other factors such as clarity, cut and color also affect brilliance. There can be some variation in the RI of a species depending on a stone's origin and color. This is because of the presence of impurities, which can vary according to the source of the stone. Thus the RI of a species may fall slightly above or below the RI ranges listed in this book.

Specific Gravity (SG): a ratio comparing the weight of a gem to the weight of an equal volume of water at 4°C. The greater the density, the higher the SG. The SG of most colored gemstones falls between 2.00 and 4.75.

Hardness: the resistance of a gem to scratching and abrasion. This can be classified using the Mohs scale of hardness. The Mohs scale rates the relative hardness of materials with numbers from 1 to 10. The 10 rating of a diamond is the highest and the 1 of talc is the lowest. The intervals between numbers on the scale are not equal, especially between 9 and 10. Ruby and sapphire rate a 9, but a diamond may be over 100 times harder. Some gems like diamond even have a directional hardness where one direction or surface is harder than another.

Toughness: the resistance of a gem to breaking, chipping or cracking. This is a different property than hardness. Jade is a relatively soft gem material (6–7), yet it is the toughest.

Cleavage: the tendency for a mineral to split along crystal planes, where the atomic bonding is weak. A gemstone may have one or more directions of cleavage, which are classified as perfect (almost perfectly smooth), distinct or indistinct. Cleavage has a negative impact on toughness. Directions of weakness that are not true cleavages are called **parting**.

Crystal System: one of the seven classifications of the internal structure of a crystal. It is based on the symmetry of the crystal structure. The simplest and most symmetrical system is called isometric or cubic. The other six systems in the order of their decreasing symmetry are tetragonal, hexagonal, trigonal, orthorhombic, monoclinic and triclinic. For descriptions and diagrams of the seven crystal systems, consult: www.webmineral.com/crystall.shtml

Materials that don't have a crystalline structure (e.g., glass) are called **amorphous.** Some gems such as jade and agate are composed of minute crystals intricately grown together. These gems are technically classified as aggregates (AGG) and are usually translucent to opaque.

Optic Character: the effect a gem material has on light. If it can split light into two rays, each traveling at different speeds, then it is **doubly refractive (DR).** If it does not split light, the stone is **singly refractive (SR).** In a doubly refractive gem, there is either one or two directions in which light is not split as it passes through it. In other words, a DR stone will behave as if it is singly refractive in at least one direction. The directions of single refraction are called **optic axes**. If the stone has one direction of single refraction, it is **uniaxial**, if it has two, it is **biaxial**.

Doubly refractive gems will have two RI's if they are uniaxial and three RI's if they are biaxial. The numerical difference between the highest and lowest RI is called the **birefringence** or **birefraction**. When you look through stones with a high birefringence, such as rhodochrosite, the inclusions and facet edges will appear to be doubled.

Besides indicating if a gem is biaxial or uniaxial, this book also gives the optic sign (+ or –). If a uniaxial gem is positive, the lower RI is constant and the higher variable. A negative sign would indicate the reverse. If a biaxial gem is positive, the intermediate RI is closer to the low RI. If negative, it's closer to the high RI.

Fluorescence: the glow or emission of light by a material when it's stimulated by ultraviolet light, x-rays or other forms of radiation. The term "fluorescence" comes from the mineral fluorite (calcium fluoride), which is noted for displaying an array of intense fluorescent colors. The presence or lack of fluorescence and its color and strength can be helpful in identifying gems. **LW** stands for long wave ultraviolet (UV) light. **SW** refers to shortwave UV radiation.

Pleochroism: the ability of certain gem materials to exhibit different colors when viewed from different directions under transmitted light. A tanzanite, for example, may appear blue in one direction, purple in another and greenish yellow in a third direction. Since it can show three colors, it is **trichroic**.

Fig. 4.4 Dichroscope used for viewing pleochoism. *Photo by author.*

Stones like sapphire, which can display two colors, are **dichroic**. The strength of pleochroism can range from very weak to very strong. In pastel and colorless stones, pleochroism may not be visible.

Gemologists look for pleochroic colors in stones through a cylindrical instrument called a **dichroscope** (fig. 4.4). One type is made with Polaroid material (about $50) and another with calcite (about $100). When you look at a well-lit stone through the correct end of a dichroscope, you'll see two squares. The squares can be two different colors if the stone is pleochroic (fig. 4.2). By rotating the dichroscope and looking at the stone **from several different angles**, you should be able to see the two or three colors the stone displays. In some directions only one color will be visible through the dichroscope. Occasionally, when viewing the pavilion through the dichroscope at a facet junction, it's possible to see all three colors at once, although normally, only one or two colors are visible at the same time.

Dispersion: the separation of white light into spectral colors. "Dispersion" also refers to the numerical difference in the refractive indices of a red ray and violet ray passing through a gem material. The dispersion value of diamond is always 0.044. However, the amount of dispersion (fire) that a diamond displays varies depending on how it's cut and the lighting under which it is viewed. Dispersion accounts for the flashes of rainbow colors sometimes seen in gems.

Absorption Spectrum: the dark lines or bands that are superimposed on a spectrum of red, orange, yellow, green blue and violet (fig. 4.3). The lines indicate the presence of certain chemical elements in a gem by showing which wavelengths are absorbed. You can view the spectrum through an instrument called a spectroscope, which examines light that has traversed or been reflected from the specimen. Many gems have characteristic spectra.

For additional information on gemstone identification, consult:

Gems by Robert Webster

Gemmology by Peter Read

Gem Testing Techniques by Alan Hodgkinson (a work in progress)

Handbook of Gem Identification by Richard T. Liddicoat

Identification of Gemstones by Michael O'Donoghue and Louise Joyner

Fig. 5.1 Thulite from Norway. Jewelry, rough and cabochons from Nevada Mineral and Book Company. *Photo by Sandy and Walter Lombardo.*

Fig. 5.2 Tanzanite crystal with some bicolor striping. *Specimen & photo from New Era Gems.*

Fig. 5.3 Natural-color tanzanite crystal mined in 1969 courtesy Pala International. *Photo by Wimon Manorotkul.*

Tanzanite

No history or lore was needed for tanzanite to become one of the most popular gems on the market. You just look at the stone and fall in love with it. From one angle it may display a rich blue color, from another it can look purple and from a third, it may be green, yellow or reddish brown. What's more, tanzanite can appear one color indoors and another outdoors. A high clarity and transparency add to its beauty. Its large clean sizes allow it to be cut into attractive large stones.

According to an official acknowledgment by the government of Tanzania, tanzanite was discovered in 1967 by Ndugu Jumanne M. Ngoma in Merelani Arusha in the area called Kiteto. A few months after tanzanite was discovered, it was classified as a variety of zoisite, a gem species of the epidote mineral group. Initially, it was called blue zoisite or sapphire zoisite. However, the name "zoisite" was unknown to the general public, and it sounded somewhat like the word "suicide." Therefore, when Tiffany's launched the stone on the market in 1968, their president Henry Platt named it tanzanite, in honor of the country where it was found. Tanzanite is still only mined in the Merelani Hills of Eastern Africa. (For more information on the history of tanzanite, see the September-October 2009 issue of the *Mineralogical Record* entitled *Merelani, Tanzania* and the book *Tanzanite, All about One of the Most Fascinating Gemstones, The True Story*, by Valerio Zancanella, a geologist who did his thesis on tanzanite crystallography and mineralogy).

In 2002, Tanzanite was added as an alternate for the traditional December birthstones turquoise and zircon. Another modern tradition is to give tanzanite on the birth of a baby as a way of celebrating the miracle of new life and paying tribute to the parents.

Other Zoisites and their Geographic Sources

Zoisite was named after Siegmund Zois, an Austrian scholar and mineral collector whose family owned an iron mine in the Austrian Alps. The mineral was first called saualpit, but was later renamed "zoisite" by the Austrian scholar and mineralogist Abram Gottlieb Werner.

Non-gem quality zoisite is found in other forms and goes by a variety of names. For example, **thulite**, which is also called **rosaline,** is pink zoisite colored by manganese. Often mottled with white calcite, it was first found in Norway and named after Thule, a place in ancient classical literature near Norway.

Fig. 5.4 Green zoisite (anyolite) and ruby figurine from Kazanjian Brothers Inc. *Photo by author.*

Fig. 5.5 Yellow zoisite from Pala International. *Photo: Jason Stephenson.*

Fig. 5.6 Four color varieties of zoisite from Overland Gems. The purplish tanzanite on the right was heat treated. *Photographed under incandescent lighting by author.*

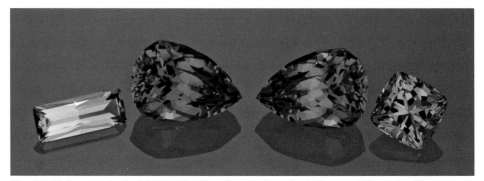

Fig. 5.7 Pink tanzanite (zoisite) cut by Clay Zava. *Photo by Robert and Orasa Weldon..*

Thulite is also found in Greenland, Western Australia, Austria, Washington, California, Nevada, and North Carolina. It's used in jewelry and for carvings.

First found in Longido, Tanzania, **anyolite** is an ornamental green zoisite, which is mined in Tanzania and Kenya. The name was derived from the Masai word for green, *anyoli.* (Masai is an ethnic group in East Africa.) Anyolite is often found with semi-translucent ruby and carved into colorful ruby and zoisite figurines and other decorative objects.

In his book *Color Encyclopedia of Gemstones* (1987, p 89), Joel Arem says that a greenish-gray zoisite is found in Wyoming and is sometimes tumble-polished for jewelry. Arem and www.mindat.org list Mexico, Finland, Scotland, Russia, Japan, Germany, China, Chile and Pakistan as other sources of zoisite.

What is Tanzanite?

In 1968, Tiffany & Co. defined tanzanite as the blue to purple variety of the mineral zoisite. Since that time, *transparent* green, pink and yellow zoisites have also appeared on the market. Some dealers prefer to call them green, pink and yellow tanzanites because this differentiates them from non-transparent zoisites.

Most mineralogists and even many tanzanite promoters believe that the term "tanzanite" should be restricted to the blue/purple variety of zoisite. For example, Gabriella Endlin, Technical Director of the Tanzanite Foundation, thinks that terms such as "green tanzanite" are misnomers. She says:

> We at the Tanzanite Foundation along with our laboratories currently grading tanzanite according to the Tanzanite Quality Scale ™ (IGI, AGTA and AGL) feel that we need to be careful what we call tanzanite. While zoisite occurs widely, it is the rare presence of vanadium that gives tanzanite its unique colour, and therefore we should always refer to the colouring agent of the stone. For example, for "Green Tanzanite," we could use the term "Chrome Zoisite," as chromium is the colouring agent that makes the stone green. Terms such as Green Zoisite are certainly not incorrect because it combines the colour description with the species name.

There are other reasons why many gemologists believe that the term "tanzanite" should be reserved for blue to purple varieties of transparent zoisite and that terms such as "yellow" or "green" tanzanite are incorrect. An example used to substantiate their view is the effort that was made to combine a color with a well-known gem variety of beryl by using the term "red emerald." This was not generally accepted on several levels, not the least being 1) the variety name already specified what color it should be (green for emerald), and 2) the coloring agent was completely different between the two colors (emerald's green comes from chromium or vanadium, while red beryl's color is the result of manganese impurities). Similarly, in the case of tanzanite 1) the variety name already specifies what color it should be (blue to purple), and 2) the coloring agent for tanzanite is vanadium instead of chromium or another element.

Dealers who think that transparency rather than color should be the criterion for differentiating tanzanite from zoisite offer the following arguments:

◆ Non-blue transparent zoisite and tanzanite are both priced by carat weight and can sell for similar gem-grade prices. *Non*-transparent zoisite is priced by the gram or the piece or bead and sells for a fraction of the cost of transparent zoisite.

◆ When the word "sapphire" is unmodified, it implies blue corundum. Yet green corundum, for example, is called green sapphire, and non-blue sapphires in general are called fancy-colored sapphires. Likewise, dealers who sell transparent zoisites that are not blue, think they should be able to refer to them as fancy-colored tanzanites, which are differentiated from blue tanzanite with a color modifier such as green, pink, or yellow.

◆ There's no practical way for jewelers and dealers to determine the coloring agents of their zoisites.

◆ Most tanzanite is brown in its natural state and requires heat treatment to achieve an attractive blue color. Emerald, on the other hand, is naturally green.

◆ The orientation of a stone is often what determines its face-up color. For example, a green zoisite crystal can look blue when you look at it from a different direction (fig.5.11). Is it fair to say that the stone can only be called tanzanite from one direction but must be called green zoisite when oriented differently? In the case of red beryl, no matter how it's viewed, it looks red.

I think sellers have legitimate reasons for differentiating tanzanite from zoisite on the basis of transparency. As a writer I prefer the term "green tanzanite" because it's shorter than "transparent green zoisite" and conveys more clearly the value of the stone, which is typically either the same or more than that of blue tanzanite of similar clarity, cut quality and color saturation.

Keep in mind that if you get a report for a green tanzanite from a major lab, it will probably identify the mineral type as "natural zoisite" and leave the variety name blank. The color will be indicated under the color description of the stone.

Fig. 5.8 Green tanzanite (5.45 carats) from Pala International. *Photo by Wimon Manorotkul.*

Fig. 5.9 Natural brown & faceted blue tanzanites. *Ring by Ginny Dizon; photo © Tanzanite Foundation.*

Fig. 5.10 Green zoisite (tanzanite) from New Era Gems. *Photo by author.*

Fig. 5.11 Same zoisite stone as figure 5.10 viewed from another angle *Photo by author..*

Fig. 5.12 Rough and cut yellow zoisite from Pala International. *Photo by John McLean.*

Fig. 5.13 Zoisite rough in various colors. *Rough and photo from New Era Gems.*

I wrote the preceding section after getting information from gem labs, dealers, the Internet and references listed in the bibliography. I noted, too, that the September-October 2009 *Mineralogical Record* issue on the Merilani Tanzanite mines only used the term zoisite for the fancy-colored tanzanite crystals and stones in the photos. Then I discovered a table that indicated the nomenclature approved by the CIBJO (The World Jewellery Confederation) for gemstones. I was surprised to discover that according to CIBJO:

◆ Tanzanite is classified as a commercial name for blue to violet zoisite. It is not designated as a variety name.

◆ Green, pink and yellow tanzanite are considered legitimate commercial terms for transparent fancy-colored zoisite.

◆ Transparency as well as color are used to designate the commercial names of zoisite. Pink tanzanite is a legitimate name for transparent pink zoisite but not for non-transparent pink zoisite (thulite).

◆ With respect to color, only sapphire (blue) and padparadscha are considered to be variety names. Green, pink, and yellow sapphire are classified as commercial names.

I used the CIBJO information that was available as of the publication date of this book to create the chart below. It compares CIBJO terminology for zoisite and corundum.

CIBJO Nomenclature for Zoisite and Corundum

from *The Gemstone Book*: *Gemstones, Organic Substances & Artificial Products—Terminology & Classification* (www.cibjo.org)

Material	Variety / type	Commercial name
Zoisite	Blue to violet	Tanzanite
"	Transparent other colours	Tanzanite with colour prefix
"	Thulite	Thulite
"	Non transparent other colours	Zoisite with colour prefix
Corundum	Sapphire (blue)	Sapphire
"	Pink-orange	Pink-orange sapphire

Corundum	Padparadscha (subtle mixture of pink and orange)	Padparadscha or pink-orange sapphire
"	Orange	Orange sapphire
"	(other colours)	Sapphire with colour prefix or corundum with colour prefix

In the United States, tanzanite and terms such as "green sapphire" are generally considered to be variety names, not simply commercial names. The American Gem Trade Association doesn't even list the name "zoisite" on its "Gemstone Information Chart." It lists only tanzanite.

Perhaps you may be wondering what difference it makes whether a stone is called tanzanite or zoisite. It's an important matter to sellers of fancy colored tanzanites because a stone labeled as green tanzanite is easier to market than one that is called green zoisite.

Appraisers and labs must discuss the pros and cons of various terms in order to know how to identify stones on their reports. Based on my interviews with several labs and gemologists, most would not identify a transparent green zoisite as a green tanzanite. In fact a few were surprised that I even asked if they considered "green tanzanite" to be a legitimate term because they consider it to be a misnomer.

It's important for consumers to know that if they buy a green tanzanite, it will most likely be identified on lab reports as a green zoisite. Although this difference in nomenclature exists, the seller did not misrepresent the stone if he called it a green tanzanite.

Perhaps the most important point to learn from this discussion is that as with any discipline, professionals sometimes disagree as to where to draw the line when defining terminology. Yet there are areas of universal agreement. If somebody sells you a tanzanite and uses the misnomer "Meru sapphire" to identify it, they are definitely misrepresenting the stone. However, considering the value and prestige that tanzanite has attained, it would be pointless for a seller to use such a misnomer now.

Tanzanite Treatments

Tanzanite is almost always heat-treated and occasionally coated with a blue cobalt-colored material to intensify its color. When mined, tanzanite often looks brownish or grayish with tinges of purple or blue. A more attractive blue/purple color can result if the material is slowly heated to 400-650 degrees centigrade. This process must be closely monitored because rapid changes in temperature can fracture tanzanite as it will most other stones.

Fig. 5.1 Coated tanzanites. *Photo by Fred Kahn and Sun Joo Chung / American Gemological Laboratories.*

Fig. 5.15 The coating's subtle iridescence on pavilion facet surface in reflected light. *Photo by Makoto Okano / GAAJ-Zenhokyo Laboratory.*

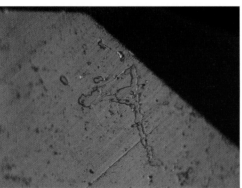

Fig. 5.16 Pits, scratches, and particles seen on the coating in reflected light. *Photo by Dr.Jun Kawano GAAJ Zenhokyo Laboratory.*

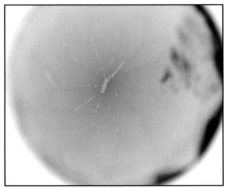

Fig. 5.17 Abrasions and scratches on the coating appear lighter in color when immersed in alcohol. *Photo by Christopher P. Smith / American Gemological Laboratories.*

Fig. 5.18 Polished tanzanite prior to heating. *Photo © Tanzanite Foundation.*

Fig. 5.19 Polished tanzanite after heating. *Photo © Tanzanite Foundation.*

The heat treatment is normally done after cutting because the stones have to be clean; otherwise damage will occur during the heating process. The color change is permanent, so no fading will occur.

It's estimated that between 95 and 99% of the violetish-blue tanzanite on the market today has been heated. (Heat treatment, by the way, should only be done by professionals. Damage to the tanzanite or injuries to people can result if done by amateurs).

Tanzanite crystals are found in a variety of other colors besides brown and gray. Some tanzanite crystals are blue or purple when mined (figs. 5.3 & 5.20). Most of these are heated to intensify their color, but a few require no treatment. Other crystals might look yellow, green, pink, orange or red before heat treatment. Tanzanite dealer Abe Suleman says that "The color intensity of treated tanzanite is commensurate to the intensity of the blues, purples, and brown before it was cooked. Yellowish and greenish colors in the rough don't always produce the best stones. Green, for example, may produce the steely blue color, and the yellow, a grayish stone."

The price of tanzanite stones is based on their final color, not the color prior to heating. The heat treatment of tanzanite is a fully accepted practice within the trade; as a result, assuming the color is equal, there is generally no price difference between heated and unheated stones.

Coated tanzanite, on the other hand, is not accepted, primarily because the coating is not permanent. It was first publicized in May 2008 by the American Gem Trade Association Germ Testing Center (AGTA GTC) and the American Gemological Laboratories (AGL). These labs had received tanzanites that had been coated on their pavilion (bottom side), which ranged in size from 0.29–4.22 carats. The small stones were immediately suspect because of their great depth of color, which is uncommon for uncoated tanzanites in these sizes. However, the coating on the larger stones was not immediately evident. Magnification was required to detect the treatment. Immersion in solutions such as alcohol or even water can be helpful. Under magnification, coated tanzanites may display the following characteristics:

♦ **Subtle surface iridescence in reflected light** (fig. 5.15). Since the coating is usually on the pavilion, this is where the iridescence can be seen. The entire pavilion should be checked, because the coating may only be on one side.

♦ **Abraded areas, holes and gaps that appear dark** under reflected light (fig. 5.16). This is where the coating has worn away.

♦ **Abraded and worn-off areas that appear light** under immersion (fig. 5.17) or when the stone is placed on a white diffuser plate or white paper while illuminated from below.

◆ **Numerous white marks that resemble dirt** when viewed under fiberoptic illumination.

Sellers are supposed to tell you what treatments their stones have undergone, but coating is not always disclosed. Be suspicious when small stones have an unusually deep color or if all the tanzanites in a bracelet or necklace are perfectly matched when viewed both in daylight and under incandescent light, especially if the price seems too good to be true. Ask if the stone(s) has (have) been coated. Some sellers will be truthful when asked, even if they don't initially disclose the treatment. Appraisers should examine the entire surface of the stone under magnification.

More information on coated tanzanite is available in the June 2008 AGL Gem Report and in the Summer 2008 issue of *Gems & Gemology,* pp 142-7.

Tanzanite Pleochroism

When you look at tanzanite from different angles, it will probably appear to be two different colors, violetish blue or purple (lavender in light colors). You may occasionally see a third color which may be green, yellow, red, or brown or a mixture of any of these colors. This is because tanzanite is a combination of three colors seen in three different crystal directions. In technical terms, it is described as a **pleochroic** or **trichroic** (three-color) gem. Very few gems are trichroic and none display the same three colors as tanzanite. This makes it relatively easy to identify.

Gemologists look for pleochroic colors in stones through a cylindrical instrument called a **dichroscope**. One type is made with Polaroid material (about $50) and another with calcite (about $100). When you look at a well-lit stone through the correct end of a dichroscope, you'll see two squares. The squares can be two different colors if the stone is pleochroic. By rotating the dichroscope and looking at the stone **from several different angles**, you should be able to see the two or three colors the stone displays. In some directions only one color will be visible through the dichroscope. Occasionally, when viewing the pavilion through the dichroscope at a facet junction, it's possible to see all three colors at once, although normally, only one or two colors are visible at the same time.

Pleochroic colors are also visible through two Polaroid filters or gels that are placed side by side at right angles to each other. A dichroscope is usually easier to use, however. If you decide to buy one, have the salesperson show you how to use it with some sample stones.

I've noticed a little variation in the way tanzanite's pleochroic colors are described. That's due partly to the interpretation of the color by the observer as well as to possible variation of color from one tanzanite to another, particularly for the third pleochroic (c-axis) color.

Tanzanite Pleochroism

Fig. 5.20 A faceted tanzanite flanked by two unheated and unpolished crystals. Note the purple and blue pleochroic colors depending on the orientation of the crystals. Some tanzanite is purplish blue before heat treatment. *Crystals and cut tanzanite from Overland Gems; photo by author.*

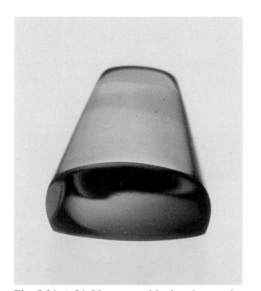

Fig. 5.21 A 21.88-carat multicolored tanzanite with three distinct color zones. It was cut in cabochon to allow each color to show distinctly without the mixing of colors that would occur with a faceted pavilion. *Tanzanite from Cynthia Renee Co.; photo by Robert Weldon.*

Fig. 5.22 From another angle, the same tanzanite is blue and yellowish. *Courtesy Cynthia Renée Co.; photo: Robert Weldon.*

Tanzanite Pleochroism

Non-heated Tanzanite

Looking at a stone in an "oriented" position, you get a combination of colors. Looking at a stone by "polarizing" the individual rays, you get pure colors.

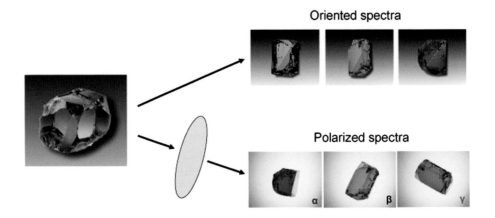

Heated Tanzanite

When a zoisite is heated, the gamma ray turns from a "mustard brown" color to a lighter slightly greenish blue color.

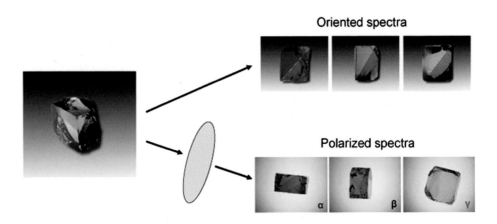

Figs. 5.23 & 5.24 PowerPoint slides from Christopher P. Smith / American Gemological Laboratories.

In addition, heat treatment can change the colors. One description of tanzanite's pleochroism is shown in the AGL diagrams in figures 5.23 and 5.24. Four other descriptions are given below.

1. **GIA *Gems & Gemology* Summer 1992, p 94**

   "One of the most notable features of tanzanite is its strong pleochroism which is usually grayish blue, purple, and brown, green or yellow. Red replaces brown in some crystals."

2. **GIA *Gem Identification Lab Manual*, 2005 p 152**

   Tanzanite pleochroism: "Strong. Usually strong blue, purplish red, and greenish yellow. Sometimes strong blue, violet and colorless."

3. ***Gems*, Fourth Edition, by Robert Webster, p 911**

   "Zoisite (Blue): blue, purple, sage green."

4. **Gabriella Endlin, Technical Director of the Tanzanite Foundation**

   "Possible colours for trichroism are strong blue, purplish red through to violet and burgundy to brown. After heat treatment the burgundy or brown is less visible as it is usually driven away under the gently heating, but often in a deeply saturated stone you will have flashes of red. (These flashes are highly sought after!)"

Metaphysical Properties of Tanzanite and Zoisite

Since tanzanite was only discovered in 1967, I was surprised to see its spiritual and healing properties described in books on crystal healing and lore. One reason for this is that non-gem grade zoisite has been known since the early 1800's, and some of its spiritual properties are said to be the same for tanzanite. Cassandra Eason, British author and broadcaster on all aspects of crystal folklore, says that tanzanite is a very magical stone that can connect you psychically with ancient wisdom, especially that of indigenous cultures whose spirituality has remained unchanged for thousands of years. Therefore, tanzanite is a good stone for guided visualizations (*The Illustrated Directory of Healing Crystals,* p 75).

In the *Crystal Bible (p 322),* Judy Hall says that "psychologically, zoisite assists in manifesting your own self rather than being influenced by others or trying to conform to the norm. It aids in realizing your own ideas and transforms destructive urges to constructive ones." Hall advised readers to place zoisite on the body or wear for long periods of time, as it is a slow acting stone.

German authors Dr. Flora Peschek-Böhmer and Gisela Schreiber say that zoisite is believed to be a kind of fertility stone that is effective for both men and women. It is also a protective stone for women during pregnancy (*Healing Crystals and Gemstones p 296).*

Fig. 5.25 Tanzanite (2.90 ct) ring. *Photo and ring by Devon Fine Jewelry..*

Fig. 5.26 Tanzanite crystal inter grown with prehnite. *Specimen & photo from New Era Gems.*

Fig. 5.27 Bi-color zoisite crystal. *Specimen and photo from New Era Gems.*

Fig. 5.28 Tanzanite crystal from Pala International. *Photo by Jason Stephenson.*

Fig. 5.29 Tanzanite ring from Timeless Gems. *Photo from Timeless Gems.*

Fig. 5.30 World's largest faceted tanzanite (525.55 carats). *Tanzanite and photo from Rare Multicolor Gems, Inc.*

Figs. 5.31–5.34 Tanzanite earrings by Erica Courtney™. *Photos from Erica Courtney.*

Crystal healers and metaphysical specialists claim that zoisite can also:

◆ Slow the aging process

◆ Detoxify the body

◆ Help heal eye disorders

◆ Dispel lethargy

◆ Reduce inflammation

◆ Encourage cell regeneration

◆ Strengthen the immune system

◆ Calm the mind

Crystal enthusiasts are advised to wear tanzanite in jewelry, because in making it visible to others, one is spreading the self-awakening that tanzanite can bring.

Identifying Characteristics of Tanzanite

The chemical formula for tanzanite is $Ca_3Al_3(SiO_4)_3(OH)$ or calcium aluminum hydroxy silicate. Tanzanite is usually easy to identify because of its distinctive trichroism. The table below will help you identify it.

RI: 1.691–1.700	**SG:** 3.20–3.40	**Birefringence:** 0.008– 0.013
Hardness: 6–7	**Dispersion:** 0.021	**Cleavage:** Perfect in one direction
Fluorescence: none	**Crystal System:** Orthorhombic **Optic Char:** DR, biaxial +; AGG	
Toughness: Fair to poor; tanzanite's perfect cleavage makes it vulnerable to bumps and knocks.		
Pleochroism: Very strong; in tanzanite, the trichroism is typically blue, purple, and green, yellow or brown.		
Spectrum: Not diagnostic: but you might see bands at 455 nm, 528 nm, and 595 nm		
Reaction to Chemicals: Attacked by hydrochloric and hydrofluoric acid		
Care Tips: Avoid ultrasonics, steamers, abrupt temperature changes and rough handling.		
Treatments: Almost all tanzanite is heated to produce non-brownish tanzanite colors.		

Most of the technical data in the above table was based on *Gems: Fourth Edition* by Robert Webster, *Color Encyclopedia of Gemstones (1987)* by Joel Arem, www.mindat.org, *GIA Gem Reference Guide,* the GIA *Gem Identification Lab Manual* (2005) and the summer 1992 issue of *Gems & Gemology* (pp 80-101).

In light colors, tanzanite may be confused with iolite ("water sapphire"), another trichroic violetish-blue gem, which costs much less.

Fig. 5.35 An example of the mixture of purple and blue seen face-up in some tanzanites, but not in sapphire. *Photo by author.*

Fig. 5.36 Note the yellow, blue and lavender colors on the pavilion of this tanzanite. It's unusual for all three trichroic colors to be visible simultaneously. Face-up the stone has a violetish-purple color. *Photo by author.*

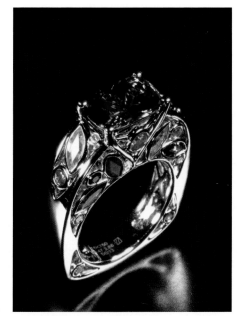

Fig. 5.37. Tanzanite ring with colored stone accents by Philip Zahm Designs. *Photo by Mark R. Davis.*

Fig. 5.38 Tanzanite pendant. *Photo and pendant from Mark Schneider Design.*

Iolite is typically bluer than tanzanite, and, from the side view, it may appear near colorless rather than purple or blue. Iolite's pleochroic colors are light violet-blue, colorless to yellow, and dark violet-blue. Its refractive index (RI) of 1.542 to 1.553 is lower than that of tanzanite (1.691–1.700).

In more intense colors, tanzanite may look like sapphire, which usually costs more. Sapphire, however, lacks the purplish highlights of tanzanite. And sapphire is a blend of only two colors—violetish blue and greenish blue. These two **dichroic** colors are easily visible through two Polaroid filters placed side by side at right angles to each other. Color zoning and a heavy, asymmetric, bulged pavilion can also serve as visual clues that a stone is sapphire rather than tanzanite. Keep in mind, though, that sapphires are often evenly colored, and their cut proportions can resemble those of tanzanite. However, the higher refractive index of sapphire, which is 1.762–1.770, will easily distinguish it from tanzanite.

So far, nobody has created a synthetic (lab-grown) tanzanite—one which has essentially the same chemical composition as tanzanite. Some sellers, however, incorrectly identify their imitation tanzanite as synthetic tanzanite. Below are some imitations and key characteristics that distinguish them from tanzanite:

Synthetic forsterite: a man-made stone that is the most convincing tanzanite lookalike. RI: 1.635–1.670, birefringence: 0.034–0.035, dichroic colors: strong blue and purplish pink, fluorescence: moderately chalky, very weak orangy yellow under LW and weak greenish yellow under SW unlike tanzanite, which is inert to both LW and SW.

Coranite: Purplish blue synthetic sapphire. RI: 1.762–1.770.

Tanavyte: A blue-purple yttrium aluminum garnet (YAG). Singly refractive with an RI of 1.833.

Tanzation: Synthetic spinel triplet with a fused cobalt layer. Singly refractive with an RI of 1.718.

U.M. Tanzanic: A lead glass. Singly refractive with an RI of around 1.60.

CZ: Synthetic cubic zirconia: Singly refractive with an RI of 2.150.

Although rare, tanzanite **doublets** (stones that are a combination of two parts glued together) have been produced, They typically have a tanzanite crown, and a pavilion of spinel, quartz, corundum, synthetic forsterite, or low-grade tanzanite. **Triplets** are also found. Similar to doublets, they are like a sandwich with a blue substance in the center. When identifying stones, check the pavilion and girdle area (narrow rim around the stone) whenever possible. Be suspicious of jewelry settings with closed backs that block the view of the bottom of the stone.

Fig. 5.39 An array of tanzanite jewelry from Hubert Inc. *Photo from Hubert Inc.*

Fig. 5.40 Tanzanite jewelry by Paula Crevoshay. *Photo from the Tanzanite Foundation.*

How Lighting Affects Tanzanite Color

The color of all gems varies somewhat depending on the light source used. However, tanzanite often shows a distinct shift of color in different lighting. A tanzanite may appear blue or violet in daylight or fluorescent lighting but look purple under **incandescent** (ordinary bulb) light. Some people prefer a strong change of color. Others place a higher value on stones that are blue in both fluorescent and indoor incandescent lighting. The following chart indicates how different lighting may affect tanzanite color. Not all tanzanite changes color. However, most of the tanzanites photographed for this book did show a distinct shift of color.

Type of Lighting	Effect of Lighting on Tanzanite
Sunlight	At midday, it normally has a neutral effect on the hue. Earlier and later in the day, it adds red, orange, or yellow making stones look more purplish.
Light bulbs and candlelight	Add red. Purple colors are strengthened, blue may turn violet or purple, and grayish colors may look brownish. The degree of change varies depending on the stone. Some stones show little change.
Fluorescent lights	Depends on what type they are. Most strengthen the blue in tanzanite.
Halogen spotlights	Add sparkle and usually make stones look more purple. The color change is generally less than with light bulbs.
Light under an	Adds blue and gray overcast sky

The whitest, most neutral light is at midday. Besides adding the least amount of color, this light makes it easier to see the various nuances of color. Consequently, gemologists like to use daylight-equivalent lighting when grading stones. Neutral fluorescent bulbs approximate this ideal, but some of these lights are better than others. Three that are recommended for colored-stone grading are the Duro-Test Vita Lite, the GE Chroma 50 and Sylvania Design 50.

Fig. 5.41 A high-quality tanzanite viewed in daylight equivalent light. *Tanzanite from Carrie Ginsberg Fine Gems. Photo by author.*

Fig. 5.42 Same tanzanite lit with light bulbs. *Tanzanite from Carrie Ginsberg Fine Gems. Photo by author.*

Fig. 5.43 Tanzanite viewed under fluorescent lighting. *Photo by author.*

Fig. 5.44 Under incandescent lighting, the stone resembles an amethyst. *Photo by author.*

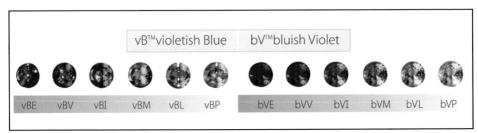

Fig. 5.45 Tanzanite Foundation's Tanzanite Quality Scale™ for color. The less saturated the color, the lower the price. *Photo © Tanzanite Foundation.*

Since tanzanite can shift color, it should also be evaluated under an incandescent lamp (a pen-light is not a large enough light source). If a written appraisal is being done on the stone, the color under both fluorescent and incandescent light should be noted. Your final judgment of a tanzanite, or any gemstone, however, should be based on its appearance in daylight equivalent light.

If you plan to buy tanzanite earrings or a piece with more than one tanzanite, keep in mind that tanzanite stones are hard to match. This is because of its strong trichroism and the differing degrees of its color shift. Due to these possible variations of color, it can be difficult to find matching stones. Dealer Abe Suleman estimates that in a parcel of 2,000 carats of tanzanite, he may be able to find only one or two matched pairs of stones. When dealers need matched pairs, they are usually forced to cut the pairs from the same piece of rough and often have to sacrifice yields to acquire the matches. Even in cutting from the same piece of rough, if a slight mistake is made in the orientation of the stones, the color can vary perceptibly.

Two stones that look alike under a cool white fluorescent tube may not match under a warm white tube. Under incandescent light, there may be an even greater difference between the two stones. As a result, when matching tanzanite, greater leniency is required than with other gems. The most one can reasonably expect from a tanzanite piece is that the stones blend together well.

When purchasing tanzanite, pay close attention to the lighting in the store, and try to examine the stones under various light sources. As mentioned earlier, fluorescent lighting usually emphasizes the blue whereas halogen spotlights tend to highlight the purple in the stone. Your impression of tanzanite color will be greatly affected by the surrounding light.

Tanzanite Price Factors

In sizes one carat and above, retail prices of tanzanite range from about $300 to $1500 per carat. In sizes below one carat, you'll probably have to pay between $100 and $1200 per carat retail. In small sizes, it is easier to find low-priced blue sapphire than low-priced tanzanite. Carat weight is a price factor for tanzanite, but it's not as important as it is for most other high priced gems.

Fancy color tanzanites often sell at higher per-carat prices than blue tanzanite because of their rarity. Bill Larson of Pala International says that fine pinks have brought the highest *wholesale* prices—$2000 + per carat. Light pinks sell for much less—as low as the prices of pale blue tanzanite. Fine greens have wholesaled for more than $1000/ct.

Yellow stones are rare, but are priced the lowest— 1000/ct is about the highest price Larson has seen except for a 12-carat gem-yellow tanzanite that sold for $1500/ct.

Compared to the other stones in this book, the evaluation of tanzanite is not difficult. Almost all jewelry-quality tanzanite is transparent and at least eye-clean. Much of it has a clarity similar to that of a VS or VVS diamond. Therefore clarity and transparency are not important price factors for tanzanite, unlike other stones such as ruby, sapphire, emerald and rhodochrosite. Nevertheless, it's a good idea to check tanzanites with a loupe to make sure they don't have fractures, which may be hard to see in dark stones.

The key price factor for tanzanite is the depth and saturation of color. Normally, the lighter the color the lower the price, as long as the stone is not so dark that it looks almost black. Keep in mind that a direct correlation exists between the depth of color and the carat weight of the stone. Medium-dark tones of tanzanite can be hard to find in stones weighing less than two carats. Larger sizes usually permit a greater concentration of color. Consequently, it's not easy for a 2-carat tanzanite to compete in color with a 10-carat stone. Stones such as ruby, sapphire and emerald, on the other hand, are more likely to have a good depth of color in small sizes. A 1/10 carat emerald, for example, may be more saturated in color than a 1-carat tanzanite.

The hue does not have much of an effect on the price. Most dealers I've interviewed have said they price their violetish blue stones the same as those that are violet. However, sometimes the bluer stones are more in demand, so they can sell for more. The hue is generally a matter of preference. You don't have to select the most expensive color to enjoy tanzanite. Many people prefer pastel colors, and they like the lavender colors of the lower priced tanzanites. They buy what they like, while paying a lower price.

The quality of the cut can play an important role in the price of tanzanite as well as influencing the beauty. Stones with **windows**, washed out areas in the middle of the stone, sell for less than those that display color and brilliance throughout the face-up view of the stone. In general, the larger the window, the poorer the cut. Windowed stones are the attempt of the cutter to maximize weight, size and color at the expense of brilliance. Some people prefer size to brilliancy. This is sometimes the case in Europe.

When evaluating a gemstone for windowing, you will probably notice dark areas in it. The GIA refers to these as **extinction areas** or simply **extinction**. All transparent faceted gems have some dark areas. However, a good cut can reduce extinction and increase color.

Before and After Photos of a Recut Oval Tanzanite

Figs. 5.46 and 5.47 Tanzanite (31.07 cts) with a "window," some chips, poor facet placement, a shallow pavilion, symmetry problems and a girdle that is a bit thin and a little uneven. *Tanzanite from John Dyer; photos by Lydia Dyer.*

After recutting

Figs. 5.48 and 5.49 After recutting the tanzanite has a stronger blue color throughout, no windowing, a superior polish, a better proportioned pavilion and a weight of 23.24 carats. *Tanzanite cut by John Dyer; photos by Lydia Dyer.*

Before and After Photos of a Recut Tanzanite Trilliant

Figs. 5.50 and 5.51 Tanzanite (18.32 cts) with a small window, a little chipping on the culet line, and a girdle that is somewhat lower in the middle than at the corners. *Tanzanite from John Dyer; photos by Lydia Dyer.*

After recutting

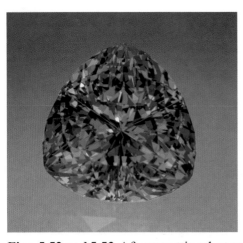

Figs. 5.52 and 5.53 After recutting the tanzanite to deeper angles and a weight of 13.88 cts, the brilliance is increased significantly and better distributed, windowing and many of the dark extinction areas disappear, the shape is more symmetrical, and the facets have a better polish and better meet points. *Tanzanite cut by John Dyer; photo by Lydia Dyer.*

One should expect dark stones to have a higher percentage of dark areas than those which are lighter colored. You should also expect there to be more extinction than what you see in pictures of gems. During shooting, photographers normally use two or more front lights to make stones show as much color as possible. When you look at a stone, you will usually be using a single light source, so less color and more black will show. The broader and more diffused the light is, the more colorful the stone will look. Therefore, compare gemstones under the same type and amount of lighting.

The quality, complexity and originality of the faceting can also affect the price. Designer cuts usually carry a premium. Notice, too, the shape outline when judging the face-up view. If it's a standard shape that should be symmetrical, check if it is. If you plan to resell the stone later on, make sure it's a shape others might like.

As mentioned previously, matching tanzanite is a challenge. Therefore, expect to pay a premium for matched pairs and suites.

Tanzanite Care

Risky cleaning procedures can often be avoided if you clean your jewelry on a regular basis. Do not clean tanzanites in ultrasonic cleaners. Soak them in lukewarm soapy water using a mild liquid detergent. Or, spray the stones with a window cleaner and then wipe them off with the cloth. If the dirt on the stones cannot be removed with the cloth, try using a toothpick or unwaxed dental floss. If dirt still remains, then have the stones professionally cleaned by your jeweler.

Jewelry care involves more than just proper cleaning. Further guidelines are as follows:

♦ Avoid exposing your tanzanite jewelry to sudden changes of temperature. If you go from a hot oven or cold sink water, or you wear the ring in a hot tub and then go under a cold shower or in a swimming pool with it on, the stones could fracture. When you're in the kitchen, keep jewelry away from steam and hot pots and ovens.

♦ Avoid wearing jewelry (especially rings) while participating in contact sports or doing housework, gardening, repairs, etc. In fact, it's a good idea to take your tanzanite jewelry off when you come home and change into casual clothes. Tanzanites can become chipped, scratched, cracked and abraded more easily than stones like diamonds. If you'd like to wear a tanzanite ring on a regular basis, choose a design that protects the stone from sharp blows. Consider choosing one with a bezel or half bezel setting or a low prong setting such as those in figures 5.55 –5.57. Avoid high prong settings.

Fig. 5.54 Tanzanite & diamond evening shoes by Le Vian® and Stuart Weitzman with 185 cts of tanzanite. *Photo © Tanzanite Foundation.*

Fig. 5.55 Tanzanite and garnet ring. The partial-bezel low setting is an ideal setting style for the tanzanite in this gents ring by Mark Schneider. *Photo from Mark Schneider Design.*

Fig. 5.56 A jewelry design that protects the tanzanite. *Ring by Shaun Leane; photo from the Tanzanite Foundation.*

Fig. 5.57 A low secure prong setting for a tanzanite cut by Frank Schaffer. *Ring by FGS Gems; photo by Frank Schaffer.*

However, even with these precautions, tanzanite can abrade over time if worn regularly. For this reason, some jewelers advise their customers to wear tanzanite rings for dressy occasions but not as wedding rings.

♦ Like most gems, tanzanite cannot tolerate heat from a jeweler's torch. It is best to remove the stone for sizing and other torch repairs.

♦ About every year, have a jewelry professional check your jewelry, especially rings, for loose stones or wear on the mounting. Many jewelers will do this free of charge, and they'll be happy to answer your questions regarding the care of your jewelry.

Fig. 6.1 Entrance to zultanite mine in Turkey. *Photo from Zultanite Gems LLC.*

Fig. 6.2 Close-up view of zultanite embedded in rock. *Photo from Zultanite Gems LLC.*

Fig. 6.3 Zultanite crystal. *Photo from Zultanite Gems, LLC.*

Zultanite (Color-Change Diaspore)

If you're looking for a truly exotic gem, consider zultanite. It's mined in a remote mountain area of western Turkey at an elevation of over 4000 feet (1219 meters). The nearest major city, Izmir, is three hours away. Zultanite's colors are strikingly different from other gems. It can change from pastel golden green in daylight or fluorescent light to a sparkling light gold under traditional light bulbs and to a muted purplish pink under candlelight or low wattage lighting. The larger the zultanite, the easier it is to see the multiple colors, which are natural—not the result of treatment.

Fig. 6.4 Left: Zultanite color in incandescent low-wattage light or candlelight; right: zultanite in daylight. *Gemstones and photo from Zultanite Gems LLC.*

Zultanite is a variety of the mineral diaspore, and the name was introduced in 2005. That year Murat Akgun, a Turkish jeweler, acquired the rights to mine the world's only commercial source of color-change diaspore. In order to distinguish it from the other non-gem quality diaspore, Akgun then gave it the name zultanite in honor of the Sultans who once ruled the Ottoman (Turkish) Empire.

Similar to the way that tanzanite was established as the gem blue variety of the mineral zoisite, zultanite is a variety of diaspore. However, appraisers price zultanite in the same way they price brand-name stones because zultanite is marketed by a single company—Zultanite Gems LLC. Akgun would like zultanite to be officially considered a general variety name in order to distinguish it from diaspore of other occurrences, which is not of gem quality.

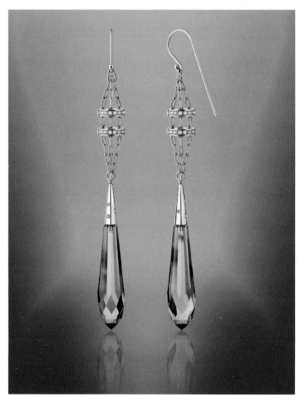

Fig. 6.5 Briolette zultanites cut by Rudi Wobito. *Earrings and photo from Zultanite Gems, LLC.*

A Word from a Master Cutter
by Rudi Wobito

In general, most zultanite rough is heavily included and not good enough to be cut into faceted gems. While the return of rough on a gem mineral is generally between 20 to 35%, zultanite yield runs less than 3%. The cutting process for this gem is difficult. Zultanite favors long diamond-type facets, as well as bowtie and radiant cuts.

When making a preform, the stone must be ground parallel to the cleavage plane to prevent it from falling apart. The grinding is a slow and meticulous process. When the preform is finished, the facets are cut and polished.

Accentuating the gemstone's inherent colors tests the skill of even master cutters who must be careful to correctly orient each crystal to maximize its color-changing properties.

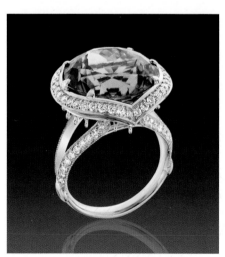

Fig. 6.6 Zultanite ring. *Photo from Zultanite Gems, LLC.*

Fig. 6.7 Zultanite ring. *Photo from Zultanite Gems, LLC.*

Zultanite Gems LLC is a strong proponent of using environmentally safe mining techniques and fair trade practices. In an October 2009 article about zultanite mining, *Rapaport* colored-stone editor Diana Jarrett says "What is noteworthy at these mines is the extent to which the system provides support for the workers. The miners eat three daily meals prepared on-site by the resident cook, courtesy of the company. They also have free transportation to and from the mines if they live off-site, but they can live free in the base camp's company-provided housing if they prefer." This is in addition to their salary and bonuses.

The mineral diaspore was discovered in Mramorskoi, Kossoibrod, Ural Mountains, Russia in 1801. However, according to Robert Webster's *Gems*, it wasn't until 1977 in Turkey that the transparent gem variety was found.

The name "diaspore," comes from the Greek word *diaspeirein,* meaning to disperse or scatter. Even though commercial quantities of gem grade diaspore are only mined in Turkey, diaspore crystals have also been found in Hungary, Chester, Massachusetts, Pennsylvania's Chester County and at least a dozen other localities around the world.

I first saw what was to become known as zultanite mounted in jewelry in the 1990's at a jewelry store in New Orleans. I was immediately attracted to its distinctive appearance and color change effect and wondered why it was not more readily available. I've since learned that it's a rare gemstone that was primarily known as a collector's gem when it was introduced to the market in 1994 by a company named Eur-Asia (*Colored Stone*, March / April 2006). After the company stopped promoting the material, Murat Akgun of Zultanite Gems, LLC met one of the former partners of Eur-Asia and became interested in acquiring the rights from the Turkish government to mine the deposit; as mentioned above, he achieved this in 2005. The first cut stones from the new mining venture appeared at the Tucson gem show in 2006.

As with any gem material, zultanite comes in a range of qualities. The distinctness of the color change, the quality of the cut, color and size are key price factors. Designer cuts typically sell at a premium. The more saturated the color, the higher the price. As for clarity, now that Zultanite Gems, LLC is the sole source of newly mined transparent zultanite, the company has chosen to market only eye-clean stones in order to enhance its image as a high-quality gemstone.

Some of the transparent diaspore on the market is from rough that was mined before 2005 and is being called diaspore or color-change diaspore. One example is the 16.22-carat specimen in figure 6.36 from the I. M. Chait Gallery / Auctioneers in Beverly Hills. Stones of this size and high quality are extremely rare.

How a Master Cutter Cuts a Zultanite

Photos and Captions by Stephen Kotlowski
of Uniquely K Custom Gems

The oval zultanite won third place at the AGTA Spectrum Awards 2009
in the "Phenomenal Gemstones" category.

Fig. 6.8 New zultanite crystals. The weight of the crystals is 1,306 cts, 714 cts, and 280 cts.

Fig. 6.9 Semi-polished crystals to view interior.

Fig. 6.10 1306-carat crystal semi polished to view interior.

Fig. 6.11 1306-carat crystal showing cleavage problems on one side.

Fig. 6.12 Side view of separated cleavage on large crystal.

Fig. 6.13 Cleavage separated from main section.

How a Master Cutter Cuts a Zultanite (continued)

Photos and Captions by Stephen Kotlowski

Fig. 6.14 Saw cut outlined to remove bad parts.

Fig. 6.15 Semi-polished removed section.

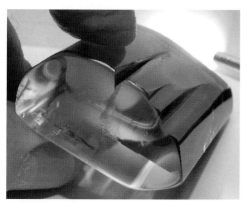

Fig. 6.16 Cleavage parting in interior at big end.

Fig. 6.17 Cleavage parting in interior at small end.

Fig. 6.18 Cleavage partings showing through main section.

Fig. 6.19 Outlined section for sawing. Center section to become 375-ct pear shape preform. Bottom section to become 53.95-ct stone.

How a Master Cutter Cuts a Zultanite (continued)

Photos and Captions by Stephen Kotlowski

Fig. 6.20 Sawn-out section of main block from 1306 ct semi-polished crystal.

Fig. 6.21 Carat weight of sawn-out sections: 375 cts, 120 cts, 56.60 cts, 25 cts, 23.50 cts.

Fig. 6.22 375-ct preform from 1306-ct rough will become an 80.30-ct oval—the largest cut eye-clean zultanite as of November 2009.

Fig. 6.23 Starting to facet 375-ct section. This is the mounted 375-ct pear shape preform before sawing off tip.

Fig. 6.24 375-ct pear shape showing problems that will need to be removed.

Fig. 6.25 Long oval showing inclusions to be removed.

How a Master Cutter Cuts a Zultanite (continued)

Photos and Captions by Stephen Kotlowski

Fig. 6.26 Fully faceted pavilion on long oval.

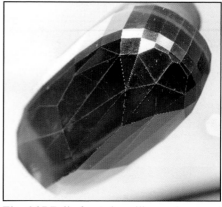

Fig. 6.27 Fully faceted pavilion on long oval 3_4 view.

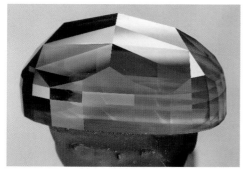

Fig. 6.28 Polished fully faceted pavilion on long oval.

Fig. 6.29 Completed faceting of crown on oval.

Fig. 6.30 Completed oval zultanite in daylight 80.30 cts. *Photo by Robert and Orasa Weldon.*

Fig. 6.31 Completed oval zultanite in incandescent light. *Photo by Robert and Orasa Weldon.*

Fig. 6.32 Zultanites in daylight equivalent lighting from Zultanite Gems LLC. *Photo: Jeff Scovil.*

Fig. 6.33 Zultanites under incandescent lighting from Zultanite Gems LLC. *Photo by Jeff Scovil.*

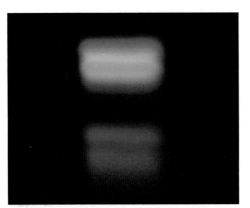

Fig. 6.34 Doubled images seen when the table facet of a zultanite is held close to the eye while viewing a light source. *"Visual Optics" identification method and photo by Alan Hodgkinson.*

Fig. 6.35 Flashes of color and multiple colors may be seen in zultanites when moved or viewed from different angles. *Photo: Alan Hodgkinson.*

Fig. 6.36 A 16.22-carat color-change diaspore. *Gem & photo: I. M. Chait Gallery / Auctioneers.*

Fig. 6.37 A 41.12 ct zultanite named "Sultan's Cushion." Stone from Zultanite Gems, LLC; photo by John Parrish.

Gemological Properties of Zultanite (Color-Change Diaspore)

Chemically, diaspore is AlO(OH) (aluminum oxide hydroxide) and may contain traces of manganese, chromium, iron, and/or titanium. The Winter 1994 issue *of Gems & Gemology* suggests that chromium may be responsible for the color-change behavior, as it is in alexandrite.

Zultanite might be confused with peridot because of the strong doubling of the back facets. However, zultanite's daylight color is a much lighter green, and it has a higher refractive index: 1.70–1.75. In addition, it has different pleochroic colors and exhibits a color change. Zultanite's hardness is similar to that of tanzanite: 6.5–7.0.

A man made color-change glass stone called Zandrite™ is occasionally confused with zultanite and alexandrite. It's singly refractive and has a refractive index of 1.532 and a specific gravity of 1.64.

A summary of the physical and optical properties of zultanite is found in the following table.

RI: 1.700–1.750	**Birefringence**: 0.048	**SG**: 3.3–3.5; Turkish material: 3.39
Hardness: 6.5–7	**Dispersion**: 0.022	**Treatments**: Normally none
Luster: Vitreous	**Crystal System:** Orthorhombic, **Optic Character:** Biaxial +	
Cleavage: Perfect in one direction making it a challenge to cut; **Fracture:** Conchoidal		
Pleochroism: Moderate to strong— violet-blue/pale yellowish green/rose to dark red.		
Spectrum: Not diagnostic: Turkish stones show broad bands at 4710, 4630, 4540 and a sharp line at 7010, similar in position to those of green sapphire		
UV Fluorescence: Inert to long-wave radiation; weak yellow fluorescence to short-wave UV. Turkish stones fluoresce green in SW.		
Stability to heat: May crack or cleave. Avoid steamers and the heat of a jeweler's torch.		
Care tips: Avoid ultrasonics, steamers, heat, sudden changes of temperature, acids and rough handling. Warm, soapy water is safe.		

Most of the technical data in the above table was based on *Gems* by Robert Webster, *Color Encyclopedia of Gemstones* (1987) by Joel Arem, www.mindat.org, and the Winter 1994 issue of *Gems & Gemology, pp 273-4. The 0.022 dispersion measure is from personal communication with Alan Hodgkinson.*

As the table indicates, be just as careful with zultanite as you are with the other gems discussed in this book. Take off rings and bracelets when doing housework, gardening and engaging in sports activities. With proper care, your zultanites will have lasting beauty.

Fig. 7.1 Petrified ammonite. *Pendant from from Zaffiro; photo by Elizabeth Gualtieri.*

Fig. 7.2 Sheet ammolite. *Pendant & photo from Korite International.*

Fig. 7.3 "Fractured" ammolite pendants by Fred and Kate Pearce of Pearce Design. *Photo by Ralph Gabriner.*

Ammolite

Ammolite is an iridescent gem formed within an ancient marine fossil for which it was named—**ammonite**. The ammonite mollusk, in turn, was named after Ammon, an Egyptian sun god whose spiral horns resembled the coiled shape of an ammonite shell.

The gem material within the fossilized ammonites was first called ammolite in 1962 by the Calgary, Alberta jeweler Marcel Charbonneau. (*Gems & Gemology,* Spring 2001 p 7). In 1975, a second trade name *Calcentine* was introduced in honor of Calgary's centennial. Ammolite has also been sold as Korite, gem ammonite, and gem aragonite. The World Jewellery Confederation gave ammolite official gemstone status in 1981, the same year that commercial mining of ammolite began.

During the 1980's a high percentage of ammolite sales were to Japanese tourists visiting Banff and Jasper National Park in Alberta. As a result, Japan became one of the biggest markets for ammolite. Japan is also a major market for opal, and the iridescent colors of ammolite do in fact resemble the play of color in black opal. For the past decade the North American market including Mexico and the Caribbean has been the number one market for ammolite. In second place is China. Japan remains a very strong market.

Every ammolite shows a unique array of color, which reveals various combinations of red, orange, yellow, green, purple, or blue. The most expensive ammolites have three or more colors and a brilliant iridescence that continually changes color as the angle of incident light changes.

Ammolite can be grouped into two general categories based on physical appearance—**fractured** and **sheet**. Fractured ammolite has a stained glass appearance because the original ammolite shell has been crushed and healed by natural processes. In sheet ammolite, little or no crushing of the ammonite shell has occurred so the ammolite is a solid mass of color. Most of today's production is dominated by sheet ammolite. (*Gems & Gemology, Fall 2009, pp192-196.*

Ammolite is sold in three forms—naturals (solids), doublets and triplets. **Naturals** are cabochons with a non-coated hand-finish, which are usually free-form. They're backed by the original shale within the fossil. **Doublets** are cabochons with ammolite bonded to a backing. **Triplets** have three layers. The bottom layer, typically natural shale, sits below a thin layer of ammolite. On top is a calibrated cap of clear synthetic spinel or quartz.

Fig. 7.4 Unusual blue ammolite. *Pendant from Different Seasons Jewelry; photo: Jessica Dow.*

Fig. 7.5 Ammolite mine in southern Alberta Canada. *Photo from Korite International.*

Fig. 7.6 Canadian ammonite pair on matrix. All colors of the spectrum are present and they are extremely bright. Each ammonite measures 12 inches by 8 5/8 inches in diameter respectively. The overall measurement is 53 ½ x 30 inches. A specimen like this sells for around $45,000 to $50,000. *Specimen and photo from I. M. Chait Gallery / Auctioneers.*

Most ammolite is fashioned into assembled stones because the iridescent layer is generally thin, 0.1–3 mm after polishing. The synthetic spinel layer of the triplet serves as a protective cover and allows the stone to be worn in rings without risking damage.

Where is Ammolite Found?

Although ammonites are found on every continent, gem-quality ammolite is only mined commercially in Southern Alberta in the Bearpaw Formation, a large marine formation composed mostly of shale. It's approximately 70–75 million years old. Most of the commercial mining operations have been conducted along the banks of the St. Mary River, in an area south of Lethbridge, between that city and the town of Magrath. Not surprisingly, ammolite was designated the official gemstone of the Province of Alberta in 2004 and the official gemstone of the city of Lethbridge in 2007.

Korite International is responsible for over 90% of the total area excavated in the past 25 years. Korite is very proud of its eco-friendly mining method, restoring the land to its original state before moving to the next site.

Ammolite Price Factors

Natural untreated ammolite retails for about $10 to $100 per carat depending on quality and size. Triplets are sold by the piece and can range in retail price from $20 to $2000 depending on quality and size. Solid treated ammolite is also priced by the piece. The following factors determine the price of ammolite:

Number of primary colors: In general, the more colors displayed, the higher the price. The finest ammolites, which are often graded as AA, exhibit three or more colors, roughly in equal portions (fig. 7.7). The second to highest grade, which is typically labeled A+, has two or more bright colors. Red and green are more common than blue or purple.

Intensity and brightness of the colors: The brightness is more important than the number of colors. An ammolite with one vivid bright color can sell for more than a stone with three or more dull, pale or very dark colors.

Rotational range of color: This is how far a stone can be turned while maintaining its play of color and brightness. The best stones can rotate 360° with a full display of color without becoming dark, whereas lower grade stones may have directional colors that are visible only in a narrow range down to 90° or less.

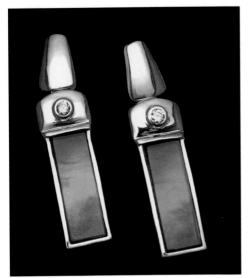

Fig. 7.7 Highest grade ammolite with at least three bright colors in relatively equal proportions. *Earrings and photo: Korite International.*

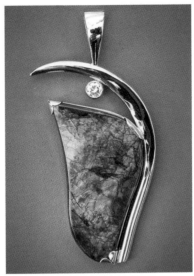

Fig. 7.8 Bright green and orange ammolite pendant by Tom DeGasperis. *Photo from Dancing Designs Jewelry.*

Fig. 7.9 Ammolite with two colors, but the orangy-yellow color has low saturation and brightness. *Photo from Korite International.*

Fig. 7.10 Low grade ammolite because it has one color and low brightness. *Photo: Korite.*

Fig. 7.11 A bright and colorful ammolite. *Stone and photo from Korite International.*

Fig. 7.12 Green, blue and violet ammolite. *Pendant & photo by Tom DeGasperis.*

Chromatic shift: This refers to how the colors vary depending on the angle of viewing and the angle at which light strikes the gem. The top grades show a spectrum of colors as in a prism. Stones that show a two color shift are called dichromatic. For example, red may shift to green or a green may shift to blue. If the color shift is restricted to hues within the same primary color group, the stone is monochromatic.

Separations between the colors: Stones with wide separations (healed fractures) are less valued than stones with narrow or few separations between the colors. Stones with broad, uninterrupted colors are the most highly valued.

Thickness of the ammolite layer: The thicker the layer the better the stone.

Solid (natural), doublet or triplet? Solids sell for more than assembled stones. According to Pierre Pare of Korite International, "it costs approximately 25% more for a natural than a doublet of equal quality. Doublets are only about 20% more expensive than triplets on average. (Unlike with opals, the creation of an ammolite doublet does not enhance the colors because the ammolite layer is opaque. It simply reinforces the material, which would be too thin to set in jewellery.) "

One-sided or two-sided solid (natural)? A very small percentage of ammolites are thick enough (3–10mm) to not require a backing. These ammolites are called two-sided solids or two sided naturals because they are entirely ammolite and display color on the top and bottom of the stone, unlike one-sided stones which have a shale backing. The average price of a two-sided ammolite is double the price of a single-sided natural. Pierre Pare says that the production of two sided naturals is very very small. It represents 1 or 2 % of all natural stones produced and a small fraction of 1 % of all ammolite production if you include triplets.

Treatment status (Treated or untreated? Type of treatment?)
Untreated stones are more valued than those that are treated. Stabilization with epoxy or lacquer substances is more accepted than color enhancement with paint or colored backings on triplets. However, stabilization and any other treatment must be disclosed.

Size: The larger the stone, the greater the price. You don't have to buy the highest grade stone to enjoy ammolite; you can find attractive stones in the lower grades. However, if you're aware of price factors such as rotational range and chromatic shift, you'll be more likely to look at your stone from a variety of angles and experience its iridescent colors. This will give you a greater appreciation of your ammolite jewelry.

Fig. 7.13 Side one of double sided natural ammolite. *Reversible pendant and photo by Tom DeGasperis.*

Fig. 7.14 Side two of double sided natural ammolite. *Reversible pendant and photo by Tom DeGasperis.*

Fig. 7.15 Natural polished single-sided solid ammolite pendant by Best Cut Gems. *Photo by Linda McMurray.*

Fig. 7.16 Natural polished solid ammolite. *Pendant by Lorne Langevin at Ammolite in the Rockies. Photo by Ossi Treutler, Jr.*

Fig. 7.17 Ammolite pendant by Dancing Designs Jewelry. *Photo by Tom Degasperis.*

Fig. 7.18 Ammolite pendant by Dancing Designs Jewelry. *Photo by Tom DeGasperis.*

Gemological Properties of Ammolite

Ammolite is primarily aragonite, which is calcium carbonate ($CaCO_3$), the same mineral of which pearls are composed. Chemically, ammolite is the same as calcite but it has a different crystal structure. The material in healed fractures is usually either calcite and/or aragonite. Below is a table that indicates the gemological properties of ammolite.

RI: 1.525–1.67	**Birefringence:** 0.135–0.145	**SG:** 2.75–2.84
Hardness: 3.5–4	**Crystal System:** Orthorhombic (aragonite)	
Luster: Vitreous to resinous	**Cleavage:** usually none visible, parting may be present	
UV Fluorescence: iridescent material is inert to both LW & SW. The healed fracture material between the panes has a weak yellow fluorescence which is stronger to long wave UV.		
Stability to heat: breaks down and loses iridescence; avoid heat		
Reaction to chemicals: Attacked by acids		
Toughness: Red ammolite is relatively tough, but blue and purple are brittle. Triplets with quartz or synthetic spinel tops are more durable.		
Care Tips; Avoid ultrasonics, rough wear, heat and chemicals. Clean with damp soft cloth.		
Treatments: Much of it is impregnated with an epoxy type substance to increase durability. It's not heated or irradiated. Sometimes triplets have black or colored backings that improve their color. Untreated ammolite usually sells for more than treated pieces of the same quality.		

Most of the technical data in the above table was based on *Color Encyclopedia of Gemstones* (1987) by Joel Arem, *GIA Gem Reference Guide,* and the Spring 2001 issue of *Gems & Gemology, pp 4-25.*

Ammolite Care

Clean your ammolite jewelry with a soft, non-abrasive damp cloth. Commercial pearl cleaners may be used, but don't use detergents or chemicals or ultrasonic cleaning equipment. Korite International, the largest producer of ammolite, recommends that you limit contact with water while wearing ammolite. Some locales have high mineral content in the water. These minerals can deposit on the surface of the ammolite and setting.

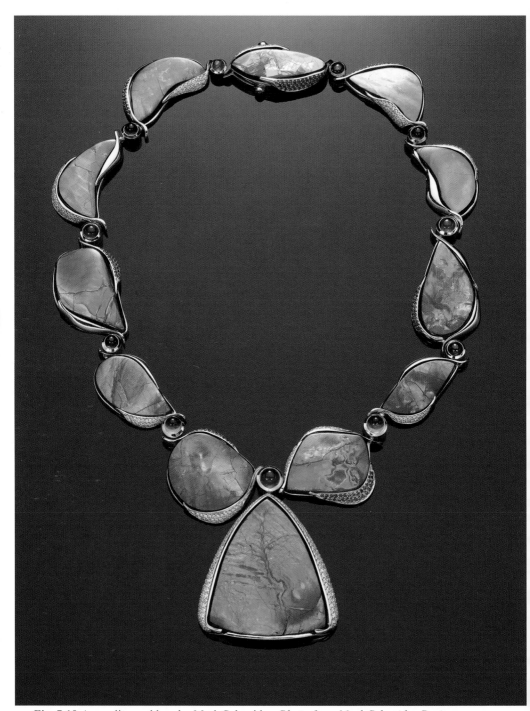

Fig. 7.19 Ammolite necklace by Mark Schneider. *Photo from Mark Schneider Design.*

Avoid intense, direct heat because this can cause ammolite to lose its iridescence. Prolonged exposure to the sun may cause ammolite to fade. If you'd like to wear ammolite as a ring stone, select a triplet. Triplets usually have a spinel cap, which has a Mohs hardness of 8 as compared to the 3.5 to 4 hardness of ammolite. The spinel cap will protect your ammolite from abrasions and wear. Solids and doublets are best used for attractive earrings, necklaces and brooches.

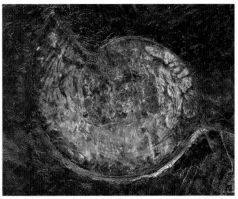

Fig. 7.20 Gem ammonite. *Specimen and photo from I. M. Chait Gallery / Auctioneers.*

Metaphysical Properties of Ammonite and Ammolite

The Navajos and Blackfoot Indians carried ammonites in their medicine bags for health and good hunting. The Indians called them buffalo stones, perhaps because of their resemblance to the North American bison.

Today, the fossilized shells are worn in jewelry and used as decorative displays. According to Melody, bestselling author of "Love Is in the Earth," ammonite is a protective stone, which gives stability and structure to ones life. It can transform negativity into a smooth, flowing energy and it can make it easier to relax while serving as a reminder of the patterns and rewards of circular breathing. Melody also believes that ammolite is helpful in rectifying degenerative disorders and that it vibrates to the number 9.

Feng Shui Master, Edward Kui Ming Li has called ammolite "The Most Influential Stone of the Millennium." Other Feng Shui practitioners have called it the "Seven Color Prosperity Stone." Each ammolite color is believed to influence the wearer in different and positive ways. A red, yellow and green combination is especially sought after because these colors are said to enhance growth, wealth, and wisdom, respectively.

Practitioners of Feng Shui believe that over the last 70 million years, ammolite has absorbed a significant portion of positive cosmic energy from the earth and universe. As a result, they claim that the gem not only brings balance to a person's body, it positively affects our surroundings as well. For example, business dealings can improve with the presence of ammolite in ones office. Within the home, ammolite is said to contribute to a happy family life. Overall, it's a stone of good fortune.

Fig. 8.1 Rhodochrosite earrings and pendant. *Photo and jewelry from Classic Colors Inc.*

Fig. 8.2 Rhodochrosite pendant by Tom DeGasperis. *Photo: Dancing Designs.*

Fig. 8.3 An ensemble of rhodochrosite rough and cut stones from FGS Gems. The specimens in the back are from Argentina. The rectangular stone at the bottom left is from Colorado and the small round rhodochrosite and specimen in the front are from Peru. *Stones cut by Frank Schaffer and Michael Spaventa; Rough and photo from FGS Gems.*

Rhodochrosite

The name "rhodochrosite" (pronounced row′ duh **crow′** site) means rose-colored and comes from the Greek *rhodon* for rose and *chrosis* for coloring. It has also been called "raspberry spar" and "manganese spar" because manganese is responsible for its distinctive rose color. "Spar" is an old name for a nonmetallic mineral. It was first described in 1813 by J.F.L Hausmann using material from Kapnic, Transylvania, which is in present-day Romania. (*Gems & Gemology*, Summer 1997, p 123)

Rhodochrosite may have either a solid pink to red color or it can be variegated and banded with different shades of pink resembling agate banding. The stone's transparency ranges from semiopaque to transparent.

Rhodochrosite was probably first discovered by the Incas during the 13th century in the silver and copper mines of Peru and Argentina. Around 1934, Dr. Franz Mansfield rediscovered a silver mine with rhodochrosite in Argentina's Catamarca Province. Further digging led to an Incan tomb containing funerary jewelry and as a result, rhodochrosite also became known as "roseinca" or "Inca rose." According to legend, the blood of ancient Inca rulers had turned to stone there. Argentina is the world's most important source of banded rhodochrosite. The concentric circle patterns are due to massive stalactitic growths in the mines. Some of the stalactites are up to four feet long. Much of the material is carved into ornamental figurines or cut as spheres. Some of it is used for beads and cabochons.

In 1974, South Africa became an important source of rhodochrosite specimens when it was discovered in the N'Chwaning mine in the Kalahari desert region of Cape Province. Transparent crystals are from there are rare, but stones up to 60 carats in weight have been cut, and some of the stones have had a deep pink to red or orange color. Most of the material is translucent. Production in South Africa is very limited now.

The Sweet Home mine in Alma, Colorado has produced much of the world's finest rhodochrosite. Intense red crystals have been known in Colorado since the 1880's, but it wasn't until the early 1990's that mining techniques were developed to recover them economically. The Sweet Home mine was operated by Brian Lees of Collector's Edge until 2004, when it ceased operation. Prices of fine red Colorado stones have increased dramatically since then. Expect to pay more than $1000 per carat for fine quality Sweet Home gems above five carats, if you can find them. Colorado named rhodochrosite its state mineral in 2002 based on a proposal by a local high school.

Fig. 8.4 Rhodochrosite from the N'Chwaning mine in North Cape Province , South Africa; found between 1979 and the early 1980's; 11.5 x 9.3 x 2.5 cm overall. *Specimen and photo courtesy I. M. Chait Gallery / Auctioneers.*

Fig. 8.7 A radiating cluster of rhodochrosite crystals from N'Chwaning, South Africa (4.1 x 3.1 x 2.8 cm). *Specimen courtesy Pala International; photo by Wimon Manorotkul.*

Fig. 8.5 A 16.27-carat South African rhodochrosite from Pala International (20.21mm x 13.41 mm). *Photo: Jason Stephenson.*

Fig. 8.6 A 16.27-carat South African rhodochrosite from Pala International (20.21mm x 13.41 mm). *Photo by Jason Stephenson.*

Fig. 8.8 Peruvian rhodochrosites (6.22 carats and 6.51 carats). *Gems from Pala International; photo by Mia Dixon.*

Fig. 8.10 Alma, Colorado rhodochrosite (19.78 carats) from Pala International. *Photo by Jason Stephenson.*

Fig. 8.9 Colorado rhodochrosites from the collection of Paul Cory of Iteco, Inc. *Photo by Jeff Scovil.*

Fig. 8.11 A Chinese rhodochrosite (7.96 carats) from Pala International. *Photo by Mia Dixon.*

Fig. 8.12 Sweet Home Mine rhodochrosite found during the 1996 mining season. The specimen sold for a hammer price of $38,125 at the Sotheby's January 11/12, 2001 New York auction and is 12 x 9.5 x 8 cm overall. *Specimen & photo from I. M. Chait Gallery / Auctioneers.*

Fig. 8.13 Rhodochrosite earrings. *Photo and earrings from Timeless Gems.*

Rhodochrosite is found in several places in Peru, notably the Huallapon mine in the Pasto Bueno district and the Uchucchaqua mine in Lima Department. Both have produced pink to red gem quality crystals that in sizes under ten carats, compete with those of Colorado and South Africa. Translucent and banded material is found in various Peruvian mines.

Smaller deposits of rhodochrosite are found in Mont Saint-Hilaire, Quebec; Magdalena, Mexico; Butte, Montana; Japan and Romania.

China has become a new source of rhodochrosite. The material has an orangy pink color similar to padparadscha and was introduced at the 2009 Tucson gem show. It's from the Wudong mine in the Wuzhou area of Guangxi Zhuang Autonomous Region. Thus far production is modest.

Retail prices for one- to three-carat Chinese stones that are eye-clean and transparent range from around $200 to $400 per carat. Larger sizes sell for more and translucent stones sell for much less. Clarity and transparency are key factors along with carat weight. Cut quality also affects the price. Most Chinese rhodochrosite is similar in color.

Banded rhodochrosite beads often cost more than many other similar stones, and the selection may be limited. Plan on paying at least $100 for a nice 15-16 inch strand of round 5mm+ beads. As the bead size increases, the price rises. Cabochons vary widely in price. The pattern, thickness, translucency, clarity, color and size affect their value.

Spiritual and Healing Properties of Rhodochrosite

Rhodochrosite is a popular stone among crystal lovers. They wear it on their wrist or place it over their heart, solar plexis or the top part of the spine. Pink is the color-expression of love, and virtually all the pink stones are believed to have energies that relate to this theme. Rhodochrosite is considered to be a powerful love drawing mineral and heart healer. It harmonizes well with other heart stones such as rose quartz, pink calcite and morganite and rhodonite. Specialists in the psychic and healing properties of gems say that rhodochrosite:

♦ Improves self-esteem
♦ Encourages self-reliance and independence
♦ Soothes emotional stress
♦ Enhances dream states and creativity
♦ Lifts depression
♦ Relieves asthma and respiratory problems
♦ Purifies the blood, liver and kidneys
♦ Stabilizes blood pressure and the heartbeat
♦ Invigorates the sexual organs
♦ Attracts new love into one's life and helps keep that love in balance

Fig. 8.15 Unique rhodochrosite stalactite cabochon from Iteco Inc. *Photo by Jeff Scovil.*

Fig. 8.14 Hand fabricated sterling silver pendant with hand engraving and a bezel set rhodochrosite cabochon cut by Mark Anderson. *Necklace from Different Seasons Jewelry; photo and design by Jessica Dow.*

Fig. 8.16 Left: rhodochrosite pendant; right: rhodonite. *Photo by author.*

Fig. 8.17 Chinese rhodochrosites from Pala International. *Photo by Mia Dixon.*

Fig. 8.18 Rhodochrosite ring by Different Seasons Jewelry. *Stone cut by Mark Anderson; photo by Jessica Dow.*

Identifying Rhodochrosite

The chemical name for rhodochrosite is **manganese carbonate** and the chemical formula is **$MnCO_3$**. Banded rhodochrosite is usually easy to identify because of its distinctive appearance. Sometimes it's confused with rhodonite, another pink translucent stone, but rhodonite typically has black patches and veins and lacks the agate-like banding of rhodochrosite. Black veining, however, is occasionally found in rhodochrosite (fig. 8.16).

Gem identification equipment may be needed to separate the transparent forms of rhodonite and rhodochrosite. Refractive index (RI) and birefringence are key factors in their separation. The RI of rhodonite is 1.733–1.747 as compared with 1.597–1.817 for rhodochrosite. Rhodonite's birefringence is much lower (0.010–0.014) and rhodonite is harder (5.5–6.5) than rhodochrosite (3.5–4.5).

The table below provides more identification details on rhodochrosite.

RI: 1.578–1.840	**Birefringence**: 0.201–.220	**SG**: 3.4–3.; Pure: 3.7
Hardness: 3.5-4.5	**Treatments**: Normally none	**Dispersion**: 0.015
Luster: Vitreous, pearly	Crystal System: Trigonal, **Optic Character:** DR Uniaxial -; AGG	
Cleavage: Perfect in three directions; fracture: uneven to granular, dull to vitreous luster		
Pleochroism: None in aggregate material, weak to strong orangy yellow and red in transparent rhodochrosite		
Spectrum: Bands at 551nm and 410nm, and weak lines at around 450 and 545nm		
UV Fluorescence: LW: none to moderate pink, SW: none to weak red		
Reaction to heat: Turns brown, gray or black and breaks into pieces under a jeweler's torch		
Reaction to acids: Its powder is soluble in weak acids; effervesces in warm HCl		
Care tips: Avoid ultrasonics, steamers, heat, sudden changes of temperature, acids and rough handling. Cool soapy water is safe.		

Most of the technical data in the above table was based on *Gems* by Robert Webster, *Color Encyclopedia of Gemstones (1987)* by Joel Arem, www.mindat.org, *GIA Gem Reference Guide,* and *Gems & Gemology*, summer 1997 (pp 122-133) and spring 2009 (pp 60 & 61).

Rhodochrosite should be cleaned in cool soapy water. Some of the banded and translucent material is successfully mounted in rings, especially when set with a protective bezel. Because of its microcrystalline structure, banded rhodochrosite is more durable than the transparent variety, which is very soft and has perfect cleavage. Expensive transparent rhodochrosite is best reserved for pendants, pins and earrings. It doesn't withstand hard wear and knocks in everyday rings.

Feldspar Group

Feldspars form the most widespread and diverse group of minerals. More than half of the earth's crust is composed of feldspars. Besides being found in all colors, feldspars often display various optical effects, which may be seen in moonstone, sunstone, labradorite and cat's-eye stones among other feldspar varieties. According to the US Geological Survey, glass and ceramics are the major end uses of feldspar. In glass making, feldspar provides alumina for improving hardness, durability and resistance to chemical corrosion. This book deals with feldspars that are used for jewelry, figurines and other ornaments.

All feldspars contain three basic elements—aluminum, oxygen and silicon, but other elements such as potassium, calcium and sodium can also be components. The presence of one or more of these additional elements, in differing proportions, creates the different feldspars.

Feldspar can be divided into two basic subgroups:

1. **Potassium feldspars**: This subgroup is potassium (K) dominant and includes the species **microcline** and **orthoclase** with the variety adularia.

2. **Plagioclase feldspars**: The members of this subgroup (series) may be either calcium (Ca) dominant or sodium (Na) dominant.

Variations in the ratio of calcium to sodium can cause major differences in appearance. The changes also slightly affect the refractive index (RI) and specific gravity (SG) of each feldspar, which helps gemologists identify them. The variations in their RI, SG and birefringence are shown below.

Feldspar name	RI	SG	Birefringence
Microcline	1.514–1.539	2.54–2.63	.008
Orthoclase	1.518–1.532	2.55–2.63	.005–.008
Albite	1.527–1.538	2.57–2.69	.011
Oligoclase	1.539–1.549	2.62–2.69	.007
Andesine	1.543–1.557	2.65–2.69	.008
Labradorite	1.559–1.572	2.67–2.72	.009
Bytownite	1.566–1.576	2.72–2.75	.009
Anorthite	1.577–1.590	2.75–2.77	.013

Feldspar group (A group of silicate minerals)

Series	Species, series member or intermediate series member*	Varieties, trade names, & popular names
Potassium feldspars (alkali feldspars)	**Microcline** (triclinic crystal system)	Amazonite
$KAlSi_3O_8$ potassium aluminum silicate	**Orthoclase** (monoclinic crystal system)	Adularia, moonstone, sunstone, yellow orthoclase
Plagioclase feldspars (soda-lime feldspars) (triclinic crystal system)	**Albite** $NaAlSi_3O_8$ 90–100% Na, 10–0% Ca	Peristerite, moonstone
	Oligoclase* $(NaCa)(SiAl)_4O_8$ 70–90% Na, 30–10% Ca	Sunstone, moonstone
Also called the albite-anorthite series	**Andesine*** $(NaCa)(SiAl)_4O_8$ 50–70% Na, 50–30% Ca	
	Labradorite* $(CaNa)(SiAl)_4O_8$ 30–50% Na, 70–50% Ca	Oregon sunstone, golden labradorite, spectrolite, rainbow moonstone
aluminum silicates with varying proportions of sodium and calcium	**Bytownite*** $(CaNa)(SiAl)_4O_8$ 10–30% Na, 90–70% Ca	
	Anorthite $CaAl_2Si_2O_8$ 0–10% Na, 100–90% Ca	

Sources: *Color Encyclopedia of Gemstones* (1987) by Joel Arem, *GIA Gem Reference Guide, GIA Colored Stones Course, Gems: Fourth Edition* by Robert Webster, www.minerals.net, www.galeries.com, www.ima-mineralogy.org.

* Oligoclase, andesine, labradorite, and bytownite are intermediate members of the albite-anorthite series. They no longer have species status according to rulings of the IMA (International Mineralogical Association).

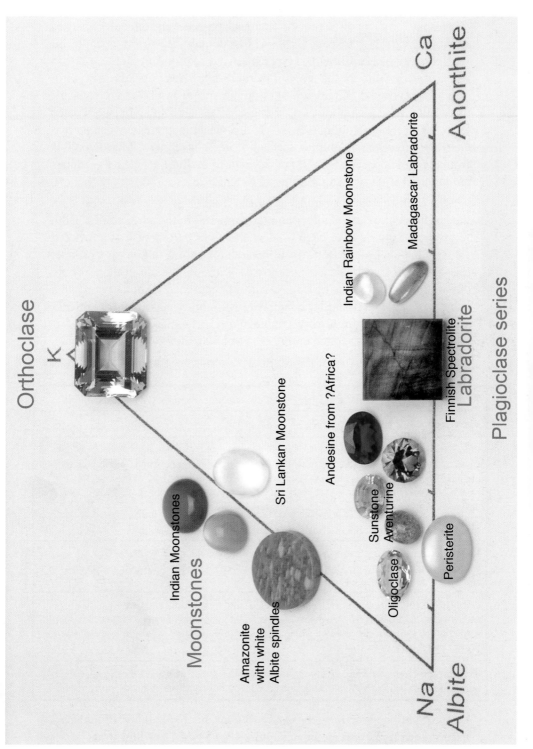

Fig. 9.1 Feldspar chart. *H. A. Hänni © SSEF Swiss Gemmological Institute.*

Despite the slight differences in chemical, physical and optical properties among the various feldspars, they are alike in many ways. For example, all feldspars can be easily cleaved (split) in two directions. In fact, "spar" is a word used by miners for any shiny rock that cleaves easily. The term orthoclase is from the Greek *orthos* (straight, upright) and *klasis* (cleavage); its two cleavage planes are at right angles. The name "plagioclase" comes from the Greek for "oblique cleavage" because the angle between its two cleavage directions is oblique instead of at right angles. "Microcline" is from the Greek *micros* (small) and *klinein* (to incline); its cleavage planes are inclined slightly away from a right angle.

The Mohs hardness of feldspar ranges from 6 to 6.5, which is less than the hardness of quartz, another common mineral in the earth's crust. Both feldspar and quartz have been used as abrasives, but the use of powdered feldspar in the cleanser Bon Ami allowed it to become famous as a product that can clean hard surfaces effectively without scratching them. Many environmentalists are using Bon Ami now because it does not rely on harsh chemicals to clean. Its hardness and wide availability make it an ideal cleanser (www.bonami.com/history/). Incidentally, orthoclase is used as a reference mineral for the scratch hardness test at 6 on the Mohs hardness scale.

Other characteristics of the feldspar minerals are summarized below.

Hardness: 6– 6.5	Optic Character: Doubly refractive, biaxial; AGG reaction common
Dispersion: 0.012	Cleavage: Perfect and easy in two directions; parting is also common.

Pleochroism: Usually none, but some transparent types may show weak to moderate pleochroism. One exception is Oregon sunstone, which can show strong green / red to pink or orange pleochroism in green stones. The lower the color saturation of the sunstone, the weaker the pleochroism. Some uniformly red Oregon sunstones do not show green in any direction. All green crystals have at least one red direction.

Stability to heat: May crack or cleave; amazonite may also lose color.

Reaction to chemicals: Readily attacked by hydrofluoric acid, slowly attacked by hydrochloric acid, impurities may be attacked by other acids. Pickling solutions can dull a stone's surface and damage backings.

Care tips: Avoid ultrasonics, steamers, heat, acids and rough handling. Clean with warm, soapy water. Feldspar's cleavage makes it susceptible to chipping and cracks; jewelers should avoid putting too much pressure on stones during setting. Remove stones during retipping to protect them from the heat of the torch.

Treatments: Normally none, except for amazonite which may be waxed, impregnated with colorless resins or irradiated, and andesine which may be heated and diffused with copper.

Information about the geographic sources, history and lore of feldspars used in jewelry is provided in Chapters 10, 11 and 12 of this book.

Sunstone

The sun represents light, warmth, energy, and power, and so does sunstone. North American Indians used sunstone in "medicine wheel" ceremonies to connect with the healing light of the sun. In India, it was once believed that sunstone was a piece of the sun that would bring prosperity, power, insight, and good health. Even today, sunstone is used as an aid to healing and meditation. However, since the discovery of the Ponderosa mine in central Oregon in1980, sunstone has become more noted for its beauty and versatility in jewelry.

Unlike the brownish orange sunstone in other areas, Oregon sunstone is found in a wide array of natural colors—red, green, yellow, orange, brown, pink, greenish blue or colorless; it may be bicolor, tricolor or exhibit a color change under different light sources. Sometimes it displays different colors depending on how you turn the stone. The color variations in Oregon sunstone are due to the presence of copper, an element not found in sunstone from other localities.

The higher transparency of Oregon sunstone also distinguishes it from material elsewhere. Considering the uniqueness of Oregon sunstone, it's not surprising that it was designated the state gem of Oregon in 1987.

What is Sunstone?

Prior to the discovery of sunstone in Oregon, the term "sunstone" was only used as a trade name for feldspars that had a glittery effect or golden sheen. Gemologists call this phenomenon **aventurescence**. It's caused by light reflecting from platy crystals of copper, hematite, or another mineral inside the stone. Sunstone is also called aventurine feldspar.

In 1896, German mineralogist Max Bauer wrote in his classic book *Precious Stones, Volume II* (p 426):

The term sun-stone is applied to felspar of various kinds which have one feature in common, namely, the reflection of a brilliant red metallic glitter from a background which has little transparency and which is pale or almost white in colour. This metallic reflection is specially intense in direct sunlight or in a strong artificial light. The points which reflect the glittering light may be distributed singly and sparingly over the surface of the stone, or they may be numerous and closely aggregated; in the latter case there is over the whole surface a brilliant and glittering sheen. It is obvious that the name sun-stone is descriptive of this peculiar feature.

Fig. 10.1 Rough and faceted Oregon sunstone, Dust Devil Mine, cut by Larry Woods of Jewels by Woods. *Photo by John Parrish.*

Fig. 10.2 Oregon sunstone cabochons cut by Larry Woods of Jewels by Woods. *Photo by author.*

Fig. 10.3 Pierced sterling silver pendant with an African sunstone carving and faceted Oregon sunstone accents. *Pendant created by Mark Anderson and Jessica Dow; photo by Jessica Dow.*

Fig. 10.4 African sunstone pendant by Different Seasons Jewelry. *Photo by Jessica Dow.*

Fig. 10.5 Indian sunstone. *Photo by author.*

Fig. 10.6 African sunstone rough used to cut the stones in figures 10.3 & 10.4. *Photo: Jessica Dow.*

Fig. 10.7 Sunstone carving by Mark Anderson used for fig. 10.3 pendant. *Photo by Jessica Dow.*

Fig. 10.8 Sunstone from Tanzania, Arusha region, 20.37 carats, 29 x 15.3 x 8.9 mm from Pala International. *Photo by Mia Dixon.*

Fig. 10.9 Sunstone from Tanzania, 10.22 carats, 24 x 10 mm from New Era Gems. *Photo from New Era Gems.*

Fig. 10.10 Photomicrograph of randomly oriented hematite platelets in a Tanzanian sunstone from Pala International. *Photo by Wimon Manorotkul.*

Fig. 10.11 Tanzanian sunstone. *Gem and photo from New Era Gems.*

After the discovery of sunstone in Oregon, the meaning of "sunstone" gradually began to change up to the point where today you may find any labradorite feldspar from Oregon being sold as Oregon sunstone. According to the GIA *Colored Stones* course (2002, lesson 26, p 14), "not all sunstones are aventurescent. The appearance of the phenomenon depends on the size of the inclusions. Small inclusions create a reddish or golden sheen on top of any body color. Larger inclusions create attractive, glittery reflections." Many Oregon labradorites have copper inclusions that are too small to see under 10x. They are still identified as sunstones.

The term **schiller** is also used to describe the glistening appearance of sunstone. "Schiller" is derived from the Old High German *scilihen*, which means to wink or blink. Oregon sunstone dealers tend to use "schiller" to describe the twinkling effect of sunstone, perhaps because it's shorter than "aventurescence" and easier for consumers to understand.

Not all sunstones come from the same side of the feldspar family. For example, Oregon sunstone is labradorite, whereas sunstone from India, Norway and Ontario is oligoclase (*Gems* by Robert Webster, 4th Edition, pp 195 & 196). As the GIA states, "the name sunstone refers to the gem's appearance rather than to its chemical composition or physical structure."

Geographic Sources of Sunstone

The most important sources of sunstone are India, Oregon, Tanzania, Norway, and Ontario, Canada. Sunstone has also been found in Russia, Finland, Madagascar, Mexico, Australian Northern Territory, Maine, New Mexico, New York, North Carolina, Pennsylvania, Virginia, and California.

The Ponderosa mine in the high desert of central Oregon is the most prolific sunstone mine in the world. Another important Oregon deposit is near the small town of Plush in Lake County, where the US Bureau of Mines has established a free, public collecting area. Two other deposits are in Harney County. These mining areas produce the widest variety of sunstone colors and qualities of any area of the world.

The color, clarity and transparency of Oregon sunstones are natural; in other words, they have not been heated or clarity enhanced. Top-grade red or green transparent Oregon sunstones can retail for more than $1000 per carat. The uniqueness and high value of these stones has encouraged dealers to refer to them as Oregon sunstones, not simply sunstones. A key feature that helps gemologists identify them is that the Oregon material is the only sunstone that contains orangy yellow inclusions of copper.

Sunstone from Tanzania entered the market in 2002. Randomly oriented hematite platelets are responsible for its aventurescence. Its properties are consistent with those of oligoclase feldspar. For more information on Tanzanian feldspar, see the Summer 2002 issue of *Gems & Gemology*.

In 1896, Dr. Max Bauer provided a historical perspective of geographic sources of sunstone in *Precious Stones, Volume II* on pager 427 and 428:

At the beginning of the nineteenth century sun-stone was a great rarity and very costly. There were only a few small pieces known to be in existence, and the single locality given for it was Sattel Island in the White Sea near Archangel. The fragments of sun-stone found here were described as masses of cloudy, white, translucent felspar, in which were portions here and there showing a golden sheen. Subsequently the East Indies and Ceylon were mentioned as localities for sun-stone, but the occurrence of the stone there is probably not authentic.

In the year 1831 an occurrence of sun-stone was discovered at Verchne Udinsk on the Selenga, a river flowing into Lake Baikal in Siberia . . . It is of clove-brown colour, and in this case also the sheen is due to scales of haematite, which are arranged parallel to the plane of easier cleavage . . .

The most typical and beautiful sun-stone was discovered in the 'fifties [1850's] at Tvedestrand in the South of Norway . . .

Sunstone also occurs in North America, for example, at Statesville in North Carolina . . . It is found at Fairfield in Pennsylvania and at other places in the same state.

Identifying Sunstone

Appearance can distinguish most sunstone from other minerals and from goldstone, a glass imitation with minute copper platelets. Some sunstones, however, may be confused with gems such as tourmaline, spinel, pink topaz, rhodochrosite, alexandrite and andalusite. Oregon sunstone's refractive index range of 1.559–1.568 and birefringence of 0.009 will distinguish it from stones that look similar.

The Winter 1991 issue of *Gems & Gemology* (pp 232 & 233), states that "the locality origin [of sunstone] (i.e., Oregon) can be determined visually by 10x examination of the aventurescence. The inclusions in aventurescent feldspar from India have a distinctly redder color, a less reflective dull metallic luster, and are an order of magnitude larger than those from Oregon."

Ev Tucker, a dealer and gemologist who specializes in Oregon sunstone, says that while many faceted Oregon sunstones will show some copper platelets under 10x magnification, a few don't show any. She says these stones can be identified on the basis of their RI and internal features such as color zoning and wispy white parallel lines along cleavage planes.

If distinct red-to-green pleochroism is present, it can be used to help identify Oregon sunstone. No other gem mineral, including labradorite from other localities, exhibits the same distinct red-to-green pleochroism.

Fig. 10.12 Oregon sunstone rough with schiller. *Rough & photo from Desert Sun Mining & Gems Corporation.*

Fig. 10.13 Earrings made from Oregon schiller sunstone. *Earrings from Rogue Gems LLC; photo by Robert & Orasa Weldon.*

Fig. 10.14 Oregon sunstones and rough *Photo: Wolf Kuehn /Canadian Institute of Gemmology.*

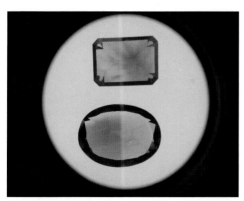

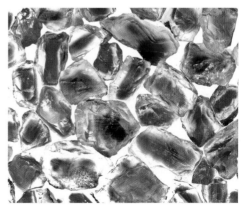

Fig. 10.15 Pleochroic colors of the sunstones in figure 10,14. *Photo by Wolf Kuehn / Canadian Institute of Gemmology.*

Fig. 10.16 Oregon sunstone rough used for transparent stones. *Photo and rough from Desert Sun Mining & Gems Corporation.*

According to research on Ponderosa sunstone by geologists Christopher L. Johnston, Mickey E. Gunter, and Charles R. Knowles, "some uniformly red crystals do not show green in any direction. There are also occurrences of two red directions and a single green direction. Unlike other pleochroic biaxial minerals, whether the third direction is red or green, it exhibits the same tone of color as the corresponding direction." For more information from Johnston, Gunter and Knowles on the identification of sunstone from the Ponderosa mine in Oregon go to:

www.swarmintel.com/desertsungems/pdfs/geological_information.pdf.

Metaphysical Properties of Sunstone

Sunstone is a popular stone for crystal lovers on cold wintry days. It's said to bring sunshine into the home and act as an antidepressant, particularly for those suffering from seasonal affective disorder. It's also been used for rheumatism. People can either place sunstone in their hands while meditating, or sit in the sun surrounded by a circle of sunstones. According to gem lore, sunstone should be cleansed and discharged once a month under running lukewarm water and recharged by being placing it in sunlight for several hours.

Crystal specialists say that sunstone can:

♦ Increase sexual potency in men
♦ Reduce anxiety and phobias
♦ Inspire creativity
♦ Remove inhibitions and hangups
♦ Encourage optimism and enthusiasm.
♦ Regulate the autonomous nervous system
♦ Ensure the harmonious functioning of all the organs.
♦ Cure stomach aches and ulcers
♦ Relieve cartilage problems and general aches and pains

For maximum benefit, metaphysical experts recommend wearing or using sunstone in the sun.

Production of Oregon Sunstone

Up until recently, sunstone has been primarily a niche type gemstone that is very popular with designers and collectors. John Woodmark. CEO of Desert Sun Mining, and owner of the Ponderosa Mine, would like to elevate the status of Oregon sunstone and market it worldwide. To achieve that, Oregon mines must be able to provide a continuous supply of the gem in large quantities. Woodmark says that is now possible because his patented Ponderosa mine is producing more than 1.5 million carats of Oregon sunstone per year in a wide variety of natural colors and sizes.

Fig. 10.17 Carved Oregon sunstone (14.70 carats) by Sherris Cottier Shank. *Photo by* A. Balthrop/Akanni.

Fig. 10.18 A carved sunstone by Sherris Cottier Shank. *Photo:* A. Balthrop/Akanni.

Fig. 10.20 Oregon sunstone carved by Martha Borzoni. *Photo by Jessica Dow.*

Fig. 10.19 Oregon sunstone (9.19 carats) cut by John Dyer. *Photo by Lydia Dyer.*

Fig. 10.21 Oregon sunstone cut by John Dyer. *Photo by Lydia Dyer.*

Fig. 10.22 Oregon sunstone cut by John Dyer. *Photo by Lydia Dyer.*

The Plush mine, which is about seven square miles and has many mine owners, is able to produce almost as much.

According to Woodmark, the Ponderosa Mine produces 4% red facet grade rough, 2% green bicolor rough, 5% intense schiller, 26% yellow facet grade rough and around 58% clear to colorless rough. It has proven extensive reserves, which will guarantee a consistent source of high quality gemstones for at least another hundred years. This is important to designers and retailers. They want to be assured, that once they establish a line of jewelry, the required gems will be continually available.

Sunstone Price Factors

Transparency is a key factor in pricing sunstone. For example, orange and gold-colored sunstone from India is generally translucent to semi-translucent and typically sells for $1 to $30 per carat. Oregon sunstone can sell for much higher prices, primarily because it's available in transparent qualities. A transparent orange sunstone sells for much more than one that is translucent. If a sunstone is colorless or pale yellow, however, the price is extremely low whether or not it's transparent. Red and green are the most valued colors. Strongly saturated orange stones can also fetch high prices. Bi-color and tri-color stones often sell for more than single-color stones.

Copper inclusions do not detract from the value of the stone unless they lower the transparency significantly. In fact, the presence of copper plate-lets is often considered desirable. Fractures, however, do lower the price. In higher grades of one carat and above, sunstones can range from $100 to several hundred dollars per carat. Large extra fine stones can retail at prices above $1000 per carat.

I asked some Oregon sunstone dealers how they price their stones. John Woodmark of Desert Sun Mining gave me a brochure with some written information, which I've partially compiled into the chart below.

Colors of Faceted Oregon Sunstone (from highest to lowest priced)

Bicolor and Tricolor	Stones with red and green are the highest priced
Red or Green	Single color red or green stones are priced alike
Orange	About 65 to 70% of the price of red or green stones, all other factors being equal.
Pink	About 30 to 50% of the price of red or green stones
Light pink	About 15 to 25% of the price of red or green stones
Yellow	About 3 to 10% the price of red or green stones It retails for less than $40 per carat.

Fig. 10.23 Oregon sunstone carved by Daylan Hargrave. *Photo from Daylan Hargrave.*

Fig. 10.24 Oregon sunstone pendant by Zaffiro. *Photo by Elizabeth Gualtieri.*

Fig. 10.26 Red Oregon sunstone with schiller from Desert Sun Mining & Gems. *Photo: Daniel Van Rossen.*

Fig. 10.25 Color range of pink, red and green Oregon sunstone. *Sunstones & photo from Desert Sun Mining & Gems.*

Fig. 10.27 Oregon sunstone beads. *Photo and beads from Desert Sun Mining & Gems.*

Fig. 10.28 Bicolor Oregon sunstone from Rogue Gems, LLC. *Photo: Robert & Orasa Weldon.*

Cabochons are priced less than faceted stones. Some are as low as $5 per carat depending on the color. Reds and greens are significantly higher. Unusual exceptional stones are priced the highest.

Ev Tucker of Rogue Gems, LLC responded to my request for information via e-mail. Her explanation of sunstone pricing was so thorough and helpful that I decided to include all of it in this section. Here is her response to my question about how sunstone is priced.

Two key factors largely affect the value of Oregon sunstone: the rarity of the material and the preference of consumers. The most commonly found sunstones in Oregon are small colorless or pale yellow stones (colorless stones are referred to as **clears**). If these are large enough to be made into beads, they have some value, although the price of the beads is mostly based on manufacturing costs. Clears too small for beads are worthless. Large clears have value and are occasionally faceted and sometimes carved (see figure 10.23).

The next most commonly found material is the colorless or pale yellow with schiller. Pale schiller is more common and less valuable than intense schiller. Next are the transparent, facet grade colored stones which can be orange, red, green, or bi-colored. Green stones are rarer, but consumers favor the best of the red material. In all colors, pale stones are more common and less valuable than intensely colored stones. And as with all gemstones, eye-visible inclusions and fractures detract from the value. Bi-colored stones are valued on a case by case basis. They can be exceptional combinations of green and red, or the colors can blur and the stones are mostly brown.

Many fans of sunstone favor the schiller material. They say the shimmer in sunstone is what the stone is about. Other aficionados say that nothing beats a large, bright red sunstone with a blaze of schiller across the table (fig. 10.26). It has generally come to be accepted that schiller is an asset to a stone so long as it's not so strong as to significantly impede the flow of light through the stone. Today such stones are usually carved. Rough stones that have significant color and schiller are highly prized by carvers who turn them into unique, one of a kind, pieces of art.

Moonstone

According to Hindu legend, moonstone was solidified moonlight. The gem is a traditional wedding gift in India because it is believed to bring harmony to a marriage. In Arabic countries, women often wear moonstones sewn out of sight in their garments because in their cultures, the moonstone is a symbol of fertility.

Moonstone became wildly popular at the end of the 19th century and was featured in Edwardian and Art Nouveau jewelry (see photos 11.1 to 11.14). Recently, it has again become very fashionable. Like diamonds, it can be worn day or night and with any color or type of clothing.

To commemorate the U.S. moon landing, which launched from the Kennedy Space Center in 1969, Florida designated moonstone its official state gem in 1970.

Moonstone is one of the June birthstones along with pearl and alexandrite. Affordable yet attractive, moonstone jewelry can fit into any budget ranging in price from as low as $5 to more than $50,000. A wide array of colors is available including, white, blue, yellow, pink, green, orange, gray (silver), brown, and multicolored. Moonstone may be cabbed, faceted, carved or engraved as cameos, and some stones display a cat's-eye or 4-ray star effect. In other words, expect variety from moonstone.

What is Moonstone?

"Moonstone" is not a mineral name; it's not listed by the International Mineralogical Association (IMA) as a mineral. Trade members use the term **moonstone** as a popular name for any feldspar gem that looks like their concept of a moonstone, yet they differ as to what that concept is. Most experts believe, for example, that moonstones must display the floating and shifting type of glow which is often called a **sheen** or **billowy effect.** (Technically this phenomenon is called adularescence.) However, there are dealers who sell low-grade moonstones at gem shows, on the Internet and in jewelry stores that have no sheen.

The website www.minerals.net defines moonstone as "any variety of feldspar with an adularescent sheen." The website www.mindat.org says "moonstone" is a popular name for pearly and opalescent orthoclase and/or plagioclase feldspar.

Jewelry Eras Starting from the 18th Century

Georgian	1714–1837 (reigns of King George I – King George IV)
Victorian	1837–1901 (Queen Victoria 1837–1901)
Arts & Crafts:	1890–1914
Art Nouveau:	1890–1910
Edwardian:	1890–1915 (King Edward VII, 1901–1910) (Belle Epoque)
Art Deco:	1915–1935
Retro:	1935–1955

Antique Moonstone Jewelry

Fig. 11.1 Victorian Brooch, Christie's East Auction 10-23-2000, $5,288.00.

Fig. 11.2 Victorian brooch-pendant. Skinner auction 09-13-2007, $881.00.

Fig. 11.3 Victorian brooch, Christies New York auction 10-12-2005, $26,400.

Fig. 11.4 Arts & Crafts brooch, Skinner auction 3-17-2009, $10,665.00.

Fig. 11.5 Arts & Crafts necklace, Skinner auction 9-16-2008, $7,406.00.

Fig. 11.6 Lalique Art Nouveau brooch, Christie's New York auction, 4-16-08, $15,000.

Figs. 11.1–11.6 Photos of antique moonstone jewelry from Gail Brett Levine's www.AuctionMarketResource.com, a comprehensive resource for antique to contemporary gems and jewelry auction sales data. On this website you can view thousands of items sold at jewelry auctions around the world and obtain gallery information, final prices, descriptions and gemological details of the pieces. The prices indicated are hammer prices, which include the buyer's premium.

Antique Moonstone Jewelry

Fig. 11.9 Edwardian Tiffany pendant, Skinner auction, 9-18-2009, $30,550.00.

Fig. 11.8 Edwardian brooch. Phillips de Pury & Co. New York auction 4-16-2000, $5,750.00.

Fig. 11.11 Ring (1930's). Joseph DuMouchelle Auctioneers, 5-3-2009, $420.00.

Fig. 11.7 Edwardian lavaliere. Dupuis Jewellery Auctioneers 11-25-2001, $4,983.00.

Fig. 11.10 Art Deco brooch. Skinner auction 3-18-2008, $1,185.00.

Fig. 11.12 Art Deco watch-lapel by Vacheron & Constantin. Christie's NY auction, 12-4-2001, $8,228.00.

Fig. 11.13 Retro brooch by Georg Jensen. Weschler's auction, 9-15-2007, $998.75.

Fig. 11.14 Intaglio ring (1980's). Skinner auction, 12-11-2007, $3,408.00.

Figs. 11.7–11.14 Photos of antique moonstone jewelry from Gail Brett Levine's www.AuctionMarketResource.com, a comprehensive resource for antique to contemporary gems and jewelry auction sales data. On this website you can view thousands of items sold at jewelry auctions around the world and obtain gallery information, final prices, descriptions and gemological details of the pieces. The prices indicated are hammer prices, which include the buyer's premium.

Fig. 11.15 Moonstone earrings by Victor Velyan. *Photo from Victor Velyan.*

Fig. 11.16 Moonstone earrings by Victor Velyan. *Photo from Victor Velyan.*

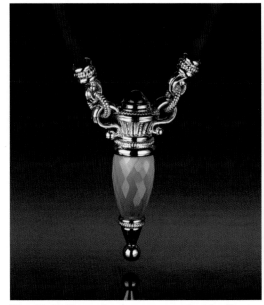

Fig. 11.17 Moonstone ring by Philip Zahm Designs. *Photo by Mark R. Davis.*

Fig. 11.18 Faceted moonstone pendant by Boston Gems. *Photo by Robert & Orasa Weldon.*

The GIA (Gemological Institute of America) states that "moonstone is an intergrowth of two kinds of feldspar crystallized into alternating layers that cause scattering of light. . . . The color of the adularescence is determined by the thickness of the intergrown layers. Very thin layers produce the most desirable blue adularescence; slightly thicker ones produce white adularescence. (*Colored Stones* course, Assignment 37, pp 10, 11).

In the *Color Encyclopedia of Gemstones (1987, p 96)*, Joel Arem says that "moonstone refers to feldspar of varying composition. The basic attribute is the presence of finely dispersed plates of one feldspar within another."

One of the most thorough descriptions of moonstone was written in 1896 by the distinguished German mineralogist Max Bauer, in his book *Precious Stones, Volume II* (p 429):

> The name moon-stone is applied to colourless, very translucent, or almost perfectly transparent felspar, which in a certain direction reflects a bluish, milky light, that has been compared to the light of the moon. This peculiar feature, like the metallic sheen, characteristic of sun-stone is not confined to one member of the felspar group, but is exhibited by isolated examples of all the different varieties. It is shown to perfection in orthoclase, and for this reason moon-stone is frequently referred to as a variety of adularia, and the appearance characteristic of this stone as adularescence. It is by no means correct, however, to suppose that this feature is peculiar to adularia, for the same reflection of milky light is to be seen, though rarely, in the colorless and transparent soda-felspar, which is known to mineralogists as albite; moreover, the same is true of felspars having the chemical composition of oligoclase, which have been dealt with already under sun-stone.

Opinions may differ as to how "moonstone" should be defined, but trade members agree that moonstone must be feldspar. If the stone is not feldspar, but resembles moonstone, then the stone can only qualify as an imitation moonstone. The identification tables in the chapter on feldspar will help you distinguish it from simulants such as chalcedony and glass.

Geographic Sources of Moonstone

The ICA (International Colored Gemstone Association) considers Sri Lanka (Ceylon) to be the classical country of origin of the moonstone. Myanmar (Burma), India, and Tanzania have also become important producers of fine moonstone (figs. 11.19 To 11.22). Other localities include Greenland, Brazil, Madagascar, Mexico, Switzerland, and the USA in the states of New York, Virginia, North Carolina, New Mexico, Oregon, and Pennsylvania.

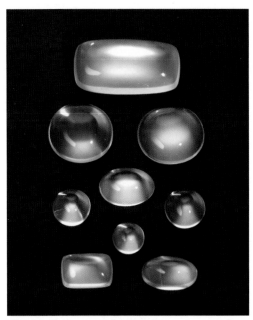

Fig. 11.19 Burma (Myanmar) moonstones from Boston Gems. *Photo by Robert & Orasa Weldon.*

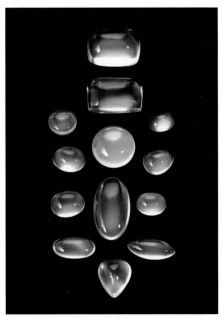

Fig. 11.20 Tanzanian moonstones from Boston Gems. *Photo: Robert/Orasa Weldon.*

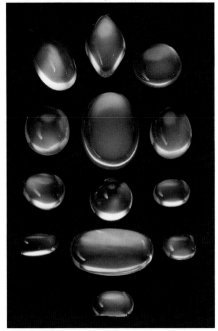

Fig. 11.21 Sri Lankan moonstones from Boston Gems. *Photo:Robert/Orasa Weldon.*

Fig. 11.22 Indian rainbow moonstones from Boston Gems. *Photo: Robert/Orasa Weldon.*

Fig. 11.23 Moonstone necklace from Boston Gems. *Photo:Robert & Orasa Weldon.*

Fig. 11.24 Moonstone from Boston Gems. *Photo: Robert/Orasa Weldon.*

Fig. 11.25 Indian Blue sheen moonstones from Boston Gems. *Photo: Robert & Orasa Weldon.*

Fig. 11.26 Moonstones pendant from Boston Gems. *Photo by Robert & Orasa Weldon.*

Fig. 11.27 Moonstone rough from Boston Gems. *Photo by Robert & Orasa Weldon.*

Fig. 11.28 Moonstone rough from Boston Gems. *Photo by Robert & Orasa Weldon.*

Fig. 11.29 Moonstones from Boston Gems. Photo by Robert & Orasa Weldon.

Fig. 11.30 Moonstones from Boston Gems. *Photo by Robert & Orasa Weldon.*

Fig. 11.31 Moonstones from Temple Trading Co. displayed at a gem show. *Photo by author.*

Spiritual and Healing Properties of Moonstone

Moonstone has been worn as a good luck stone and as a protective amulet for travelers, especially at night. Supposedly, if you place it in the glove compartment of your car, it will help you avoid accidents and road rage.

Moonstone is said to have a calming effect when worn as a pendant, while at the same time increasing your psychic powers. Try placing a moonstone on your brow before you go to sleep, and repeat a question several times to yourself. The answer may appear in a dream. Some believe that a dish of moonstones in a room can help ease the stress of everyday life.

Gemstone lore says that the most powerful time to use and recharge the energy of the moonstone is in a full moon. Simply place the moonstone(s) in a dish under the light of the moon. The resulting energy helps balance internal hormone cycles with nature's rhythms. You'll be reminded that as the moon waxes and wanes, so everything is part of a cycle of change.

Crystal healers claim that moonstone can also:

♦ Relieve PMS

♦ Heal disorders of the upper digestive tract that are due to stress

♦ Increase fertility

♦ Cure disorders of the reproductive organs

♦ Help children establish a regular sleep pattern.

If your spouse or lover is mad at you, consider giving him or her a gift of moonstone jewelry. Moonstone is believed to be very powerful at reuniting lovers who have quarreled. It's also said that if you give your lover a moonstone necklace during a full moon, you'll always have passion for each other.

Judging Moonstone Quality

The strength and color of the soft glow of moonstone—its adularescence—is a key value factor for moonstone because this sheen is what distinguishes moonstone from other gems. A strong blue sheen is considered the most valuable. A rainbow coloration is second in terms of value, and a silver sheen is third.

The most expensive moonstones have the following characteristics:

1. **A broad well-centered sheen that's blue, silver, or multicolored** like a rainbow. The stronger the sheen and blue color are, the more valuable the moonstone. The sheen should be visible from various viewing angles, not just from the top of the stone.

2. **A transparency ranging from semi-transparent to almost translucent.** Curiously, moonstones with high transparency sell for less than those that are semi-transparent. Barbara Lawrence of Boston Gems says this is because customers want stones that look like moonstones, not clear quartz. In addition, they don't want to see their skin through the moonstone when wearing it; they prefer to see a blue sheen.

Fig. 11.32 Moonstone with an ideal color and transparency from Hubert Gems. *Photo by author.*

3. **A colorless to near colorless body color**. Yellow and brown tints usually lower the price.

4. **A flawless to near flawless appearance**

5. **A cabochon cut.** Unlike most other gems, high quality cabochons generally sell for more than faceted moonstones, which are often cut from lower-grade clear material with little adularescence. Well-cut faceted moonstones don't have "windows" (a see-through effect), and they have enough brilliance to make an attractive stone. Occasionally, faceted moonstones have a high blue adularescence. In these cases, cutters may charge more than if the material were fashioned as a cab.

6. **A symmetrical shape and a rounded profile** that is not too flat if they are cabochons. Well-cut and polished stones with rounded domes typically display a stronger sheen than flattish stones. Large sizes above 9x7 mm tend to be free-form and are priced per carat. Top quality stones can retail for more than $300 per carat.

When selecting a loose moonstone, Barbara Lawrence of Boston Gems recommends that you be aware of the end purpose for the stone. For example, the stone may have great adularescence for a ring, but if you turn the stone for a pendant mounting the sheen may disappear.

The lowest-priced moonstones have the following traits:

1. **No sheen or hardly any sheen**. The sheen may only be visible within a restricted range of viewing angles. Moonstones of this quality sell for as little as $1 per carat.

2. **A transparency ranging from translucent to nearly opaque**. Translucent stones can be attractive, but usually the lower the transparency of a stone, the lower its price.

3. **Body colors other than blue, white or colorless**. The lowest priced colors are brown, gray, yellow and black. Moonstones may also have an orangy or green body color.

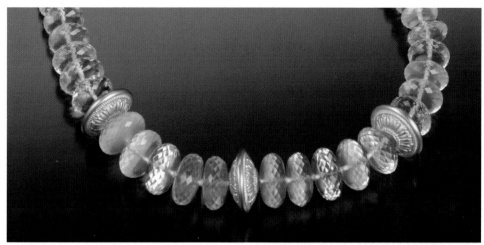

Fig. 11.33 Faceted moonstone bead necklace from Boston Gems. *Photo: Robert / Orasa Weldon.*

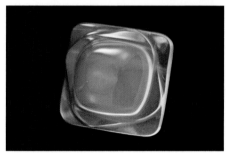

Fig. 11.35 Moonstone cut by Sherris Cottier Shank. *Photo by* A. Balthrop /Akanni.

Fig. 11.34 Moonstone brooch from Paula Crevoshay. *Photo from Paula Crevoshay.*

Fig. 11.35 Rainbow moonstones from Boston Gems. *Photo by Robert & Orasa Weldon.*

Fig. 11.37 Moonstone displaying a gray twinning plane and an iridescent green-blue sheen in the face-up position. *Photo by author.*

4. **Eye-visible inclusions or fractures**. The more noticeable and distracting the flaws, the lower the price. Moonstones with fractures are most suitable for pendants, earrings and brooches.

5. **A poor polish and unsymmetrical proportions.** Moonstones should be well-cut and polished to maximize their beauty. Low-quality faceted moonstones often have windows (a see-through effect).

A moonstone does not have to be of high quality to be attractive in jewelry. An example of this is figure 11.37. I bought this moonstone ring at a gem show because I liked its strong iridescent green-blue sheen. The price was low because the stone is translucent and has a gray line (twinning plane) across it (the sterling silver ring cost less than $50). Nevertheless, I've received a lot of compliments on the ring.

On the other hand, if you're looking for a special gift and you want to impress the recipient, you should buy moonstones of high quality. Top quality moonstones hold their value better than those of lower quality and they can become heirloom pieces. In September 2009, an Edwardian platinum moonstone pendant signed by Louis Comfort Tiffany sold for $30,550 at a Skinner auction (see figure 11.9). It was accented with wire work florets, but no diamonds.

Caring for Moonstone

Moonstone requires the same care as other feldspars. Avoid rough handling and heat. It cannot withstand the heat from a jeweler's torch. Therefore, the stone should usually be removed during repairs. Sometimes moonstones are backed with a black coating to enhance the stone's adularescence. The backing can be scratched, and ultrasonics or steam cleaning can damage it. The safest way to clean moonstone is with warm soapy water and a soft cloth. Even if the stone has no backing, it's best to avoid ultrasonics and steamers. The heat can make it crack or cleave, and ultrasonics can cause existing cracks to expand.

Gemologists normally advise consumers against wearing moonstones and other feldspars in everyday rings because of their tendency to cleave and chip when hit hard. While researching and writing this book, I've worn a moonstone ring daily without any negative consequences. However, it's bezel set with a protective band of metal surrounding it. Had it been in a high-prong setting, the stone may have been damaged with rough wear.

It's best to wear expensive moonstones in pendants, earrings, and brooches, where they are not subject to hard knocks. Nevertheless, moonstone adularescence is enhanced with the movement of the hand. If you'd like a moonstone ring, select one with a sturdy mounting and setting. Take it off when participating in activities such as contact sports, housework and gardening. Proper care is the key to lasting beauty.

Other Feldspars

Moonstone and sunstone are popular gem-quality feldspars, but other feldspars are also used for jewelry, figurines and a variety of decorative ornaments. This chapter will discuss and illustrate the following feldspars.

♦ Labradorite (labradorescent variety)

♦ Yellow or golden labradorite (transparent)

♦ Andesine

♦ Amazonite

♦ Orthoclase (transparent)

♦ Oligoclase (transparent)

♦ Bytownite

Labradorite (Labradorescent Variety)

Labradorite is a plagioclase feldspar whose beauty may be overlooked if not viewed from the proper position. It typically has a dark brown to gray color until its colorful play of light displays metallic blue, violet, green, orange or yellow hues and occasionally the full color spectrum. This optical effect, which is appropriately called **labradorescence**, is seen when viewed along its cleavage planes. Essayist Ralph Waldo Emerson made reference to this phenomenon when he wrote "A man is like a bit of Labrador spar, which has no luster as you turn it in your hand until you come to a particular angle; then it shows deep and beautiful colors." (*Essays Second Series.*II. Experience).

Labradorescent feldspar is mined in Labrador (Nain, Tabor Island), Finland, Newfoundland, Norway, Russia, Romania, Madagascar, and New South Wales, Australia. A few specimens have been found in the Adirondack Mountains of upstate New York (www.minerals.net).

Labradorite, was named after the peninsula of Labrador in Canada, where it was first discovered ("Labrador" + "ite" means rock or mineral of Labrador). The GIA Colored Stones Course (2002) says that a missionary discovered this unusual feldspar off the coast of Labrador around 1770.

Fig. 12.1 Labradorite necklace by Margit Haupt. *Photo by John Haupt.*

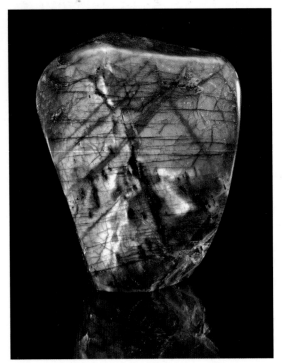

Fig. 12.2 Labradorite from Madagascar. *Specimen and photo from I. M. Chait Gallery / Auctioneers.*

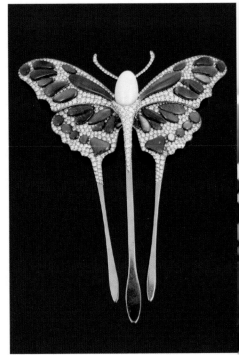

Fig. 12.3 Labradorite dragonfly created by Busatti. *Photo from Luca Busatti.*

Fig. 12.4 Labradorite hummingbirds on rock crystal. *Specimen & photo from Chait I. M. Chait Gallery Auctioneers.*

Fig. 12.5 Madagascar labradorite box & photo: I. M. Chait Gallery / Auctioneers.

Another type of labradorite from Finland is called **spectrolite** because of its vivid flashes of spectral colors. Many in the trade think the term "spectrolite" should be reserved for labradorite from Scandinavia, but some call any labradorite with varied and intense colors, spectrolite. Because of its brightness and its range of phenomenal color, spectrolite is generally regarded as the most desirable labradorescent feldspar.

Labradorite is plentiful and reasonably priced, but not well known. You can find a nice distinctive pendant for less than $100. The key selection criteria should be the brilliance and obviousness of the labradorescence. The color of the effect is a matter of preference, but generally stones that display a range of colors are most appreciated.

Labradorite is often used as a carving material (fig. 12.4). In Scandinavia, builders sometimes add decorative wall tiles of phenomenal labradorite to their interior designs for a richly patterned look. It is universally used as a building facing stone and for kitchen counter tops. Sliced slabs are sometimes displayed by dealers in water, which enhances their labradorescence.

Metaphysical properties have long been ascribed to labradorite. Bestselling author Judy Hall says in her *Crystal Bible* that labradorite deflects unwanted energies from the aura and connects with universal energies. In *Love is in the Earth,* crystal specialist Melody says that "labradorescence is a luminescence, derived from extraterrestrial origin, which is enclosed in the mineral to bring the galactic evolved energies from other worlds to the Earth plane." Metaphysical practitioners say that when placed on the body, labradorite can:

◆ Energize the imagination, bringing up new ideas
◆ Relieve stress
◆ Lower blood pressure
◆ Balance hormones
◆ Assist in digestion and metabolism

Yellow or Golden Labradorite

Chapter 10 discussed transparent yellow labradorite from Oregon, which often contain platelets of copper that reflect light. It's called Oregon sunstone. Yellow labradorite without reflecting inclusions is usually called yellow or golden labradorite.

Golden labradorite is found in northern Mexico, Millard County, Utah, and the Hogarth Range, New South Wales. Most of it is a very pale yellow and not often used as a gemstone. Seldom found in jewelry, this budget-priced stone is promoted by crystal enthusiasts for its metaphysical properties. They say it increases inner strength, endurance and courage and helps heal the stomach, liver and gall bladder.

Fig. 12.6 Spectrolite from Different Seasons Jewelry. *Photo by Jessica Dow.*

Fig. 12.7 Spectrolite from Different Seasons Jewelry. *Photo by Jessica Dow.*

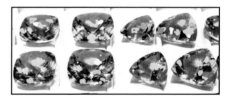

Fig. 12.8 Yellow labradorite from Mexico.

Fig. 12.9 Reversible spectrolite pendant by Mark Anderson and Jessica Dow of Different Seasons Jewelry. *Photo by Jessica Dow.*

Fig. 12.10 Reverse side of spectrolite pendant in figure 12.9. *Photo by Jessica Dow.*

Fig. 12.13 Labradorite (rainbow moonstone) from Boston Gems. *Photo by Robert & Orasa Weldon.*

Figs. 12.11 & 12.12 Both sides of a reversible spectrolite pendant by Mark Anderson and Jessica Dow of Different Seasons Jewelry. *Photos by Jessica Dow.*

Fig. 12.14 Spectrolite. *H. A. Hänni ©️ SSEF Swiss Gemmological Institute.*

Fig. 12.15 Spectrolite ring by Jessica Dow and Mark Anderson. *Photo by Jessica Dow.*

Fig. 12.16 Labradorites (Oregon sunstone). *Gems and photo from Desert Sun Mining & Gems.*

The January 2009 issue of *Gems & Jewellery* featured an impressive diamond and golden labradorite "Cup of David" designed by Joanna Angelett to represent Australia in the Jerusalem 3000 Exhibition. Golden labradorite was selected because a transparent Australian gem with excellent clarity and a golden hue was needed. Angelett couldn't find the stone available for sale, so she went to North South Wales and dug it herself.

Rainbow moonstone, another type of labradorite, was discussed in Chapter 11 and labradorite from Oregon was discussed in Chapter 10. They are shown again in figures 12.13 and 12.16.

Andesine

Prior to 2002, Andesine was known primarily as a rock forming plagioclase feldspar, which was named after the Andes Mountains in South America. The chemical formula for all plagioclase feldspar members is $(NaCa)(SiAl)_4O_8$.). Andesine has been arbitrarily defined by the ratio of 50–70% sodium (Na) to 50–30% calcium (Ca) in its chemical composition, whereas the ratio for labradorite is 30–50% sodium and 70–50% calcium.

The spring 2002 issue of *Gems & Gemology* (pp 94–95) reported that red andesine resembling red Oregon sunstone had been offered for sale in Tucson. It was said to be from the Democratic Republic of Congo.

According to the winter 2008 issue of *Gems & Gemology* (pp 369–373), a red andesine called Tibetan sunstone began to appear on the market in late 2005. It was reportedly from Nyima in Central Tibet. Later in February 2007, a similar red andesine called Lazasine was unveiled at the Tucson gem show. This significantly raised the value of the stone. A large supply of red andesine allegedly from China was offered for sale as an official gemstone of the summer 2008 Olympics Games in China. Despite claims that its color was natural, there has been suspicion that the Chinese red andesine stones are diffusion treated to produce their red color.

Initially some gemologists identified the andesine as natural because they saw no indication that it was treated and they didn't have much experience identifying andesine. Unlike diffusion-treated sapphire, where the color tends to be concentrated near the surface of the stone, the color in andesine rough was concentrated in the center. The GIA did not want to identify the andesines as treated until they could prove that it was possible to enhance their color by a treatment process. Once before, they had suspected that some sapphires that displayed unusual color zoning under immersion had been diffusion-treated, when in fact they hadn't.

Since 2008, research has demonstrated that the Chinese red and green andesine offered in the marketplace could have been produced by copper diffusion. Dr. John Emmett of Crystal Chemistry, Dr. George Rossman at the California Institute of Technology, the GIA and others have successfully diffused copper into plagioclase feldspar on an experimental basis. However this doesn't prove that the red andesine is treated. Gem laboratories still have to find a reliable way to distinguish between treated and untreated andesine. This does not appear to be a high priority for them because very little andesine is brought to them for testing. Labs have limited time and money for research, and they would rather reserve it for gems that are more widely purchased by consumers.

In the meantime, smart vendors are now identifying their andesines as diffusion-treated even if they may not be. Some call them andesine labradorites instead of andesines. Either term is acceptable. Oregon sunstone dealers call their red and green labradorites Oregon sunstones. They can be differentiated from andesine on the basis of their RI and internal features.

Color, clarity and transparency are major price factors for andesine. Pale yellow stones can be found for less than five dollars a carat. Highly saturated red stones with high clarity and transparency have sold for a few hundred dollars per carat. Translucent and pale stones are the lowest priced.

Amazonite

Amazonite is a green to greenish blue variety of microcline feldspar (microcline can also be white, pink, red, yellow or gray). Opinions are divided as to the derivation of its name. Some say it was named after the Amazon warrior women of Greek mythology. Others say it was named after the Amazon River Basin in Brazil; the stone is found in Brazil, although not near the Amazon. Another possibility is that Indians along the Amazon may have worn amazonite necklaces when the German naturalist Alexander von Humboldt explored the area and collected mineral specimens. Others think amazonite got its name because of its distinctive blue-green color, which mirrors the hues of the Amazon river and surrounding rain forest. In 1896, German mineralogist Max Bauer wrote in *Precious Stones, Volume II.*

> The name amazon-stone was first given in the middle of the eighteenth century to a green stone from the Amazon river in South America. It appears to be doubtful whether this was the same substance as that to which the name now refers; more probably it was nephrite, jadeite, or some other green mineral, for nothing is known at the present day of the occurrence of verdigris-green felspar in this region.

Also named **amazon stone**, amazonite is non transparent, it often has grid-like white streaks and an irregular color distribution, and it occasionally displays a faint sheen or aventuresence (a glittery effect similar to sunstone). Amazonite is an attractive alternative to turquoise because its color is similar.

Fig. 12.17 Andesine. *H. A. Hänni © SSEF Swiss Gemmological Institute.*

Fig. 12.18 Amazonite. *H. A. Hänni © SSEF Swiss Gemmological Institute.*

Fig. 12.19 Orthoclase (18.80 cts) cut by John Dyer. *Photo by John Dyer.*

Fig. 12.20 Orthoclase (35.72 cts) cut by Sherris Cottier Shank. *Photo: A. Balthrop/Akanni.*

Fig. 12.21 Oligoclase (8.95 cts) cut by John Dyer. *Photo by Lydia Dyer.*

One of the earliest sources of amazonite is near Minsk, Russia in the Ural Mountains. The most important American locality is the Pikes Peak area of Colorado. In fact, sometimes it's incorrectly called Pikes Peak jade or Colorado jade. Amazonite is also mined in India, Canada, Madagascar, Brazil, Norway, Tanzania, Kenya, and Namibia.

Besides being confused with jade, amazonite may be mistaken for turquoise, chrysoprase, and serpentine. They can be separated by appearance, magnification, refractive index (1.522 to 1.530 for amazonite), specific gravity (2.56) and possibly fluorescence. Amazonite is inert to a weak yellowish green under long-wave UV and inert to short-wave UV. Amazonite rough can be easily distinguished from the above by its excellent cleavage in two directions.

The *GIA Gem Reference Guide* (p 102) says that amazonite may be impregnated with wax to hide cleavage cracks that break the surface of the stone. Moderately stable, this treatment is common on tumbled stones and can be detected with a hot point or infrared spectroscopy. White microcline is occasionally irradiated to produce blue amazonite. The treatment is undetectable and stable, provided that the stone is not heated above 300°C. In general, you should keep amazonite away from the heat because it may crack, cleave or lose color, as is true with all feldspars and many other gems. Also, avoid acids.

Amazonite is worn in jewelry in the form of cabochons, cameos, beads and faceted briolettes or used for objects such as boxes, ashtrays, pyramids and spheres. Tumbled stones can be purchased for less than a dollar a stone. Designer amazonite jewelry can sell for as much as a few hundred dollars. Stones with high color saturation and an even color distribution are the most highly valued.

Gems & Crystals (p 128) from the American Museum of Natural History states that amazonite was widely used in Egyptian, Mesopotamian and Indian jewelry; some examples date back to the third millennium B.C. A carved scarab and an amazonite-inlaid ring were among the jewels of King Tut. The 23rd chapter of the Egyptian *Book of the Dead* was engraved on amazonite.

The Hebrews treasured this feldspar, and it is generally accepted that the third stone in Moses' breastplate was amazonite. In Central and South America, pre-Columbian adornments contained amazonite.

Amazonite has been called a stone of courage. According to gem lore, when worn as an amulet, it protects you from harm, gives you confidence and fills your heart with determination to do good for the world. When placed under a pillow, it can help you get a good night's rest. It's said to stimulate the heart and throat chakras.

Fig. 12.22 Orthoclase cut by Sherris Cottier Shank. *Photo by A. Balthrop/Akanni.*

Fig. 12.23 Oligoclase (7.98 cts) cut by John Dyer. *Photo by John Dyer.*

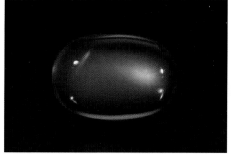

Fig. 12.24. Faceted orthoclase moonstones from Boston Gems. *Photo by Robert and Orasa Weldon.*

Fig. 12.25 Orthoclase moonstone from Boston Gems. *Photo by Robert and Orasa Weldon.*

Fig. 12.26 Oligoclase Tanzanian sunstone from Pala International. *Photo by Mia Dixon.*

Fig. 12.27 Bytownite. *Rough & photo from New Era Gems.*

Metaphysical writers say that amazonite also:

◆ Improves ones ability to interact with others.

◆ Soothes the nerves

◆ Helps you be in the right place at the right time

◆ Activates lazy teenagers

◆ Alleviates headaches and migraines when worn as a necklace

Orthoclase (Transparent)

Chapter 11 discussed orthoclase moonstone. A transparent variety of orthoclase is also available. The largest specimens are usually yellow and come from Madagascar, but it may also be colorless, gray, or greenish. The yellow color is due to the presence of iron. The more intense the color, the more valuable the stone. The stone is considered a collector's stone. Large faceted yellow stones above a hundred carats are displayed in major museums. Sources of transparent orthoclase include Myanmar, Kenya and Sri Lanka. According to mineralogist John White, the source of yellow orthoclase in Madagascar dried up about 50 years ago.

Yellow orthoclase may be confused with chrysoberyl, citrine quartz, yellow beryl, scapolite, and topaz. Key distinguishing features for yellow orthoclase include refractive index (1.518–1.526), birefringence (0.005–0.008), possibly spectrum (broad bands at approximately 420 nm and 448 nm) and possibly fluorescence (inert to weak reddish orange under long wave and short wave illumination.

Oligoclase (Transparent)

Oligoclase is a plagioclase feldspar, which is best known for its sunstone and moonstone varieties. However, a non-phenomenal transparent oligoclase is found in North Carolina, Kenya and Tanzania. Its color ranges from colorless to pale green or green-blue. Examples of faceted transparent oligoclase are shown in figures 12.21 and 12.23. Don't expect to find one at your local jewelry store or rock shop. Transparent oligoclase is rare.

Bytownite

Bytownite is another rare plagioclase feldspar, which is transparent to translucent. Its color is usually pale yellow, gray, white, colorless, or light brown, but occasionally it is reddish. The chemical formula for bytownite is the same as that of the other intermediate members of the plagioclase series— $(Ca,Na)(SiAl)_4O_8$.

However, the ratio of sodium to calcium in bytownite is 10–30% sodium versus 90–70% calcium. See Chapter 9 for charts comparing the members of the plagioclase series.

Sources of bytownite include Mexico, Scotland, England, Sweden, Japan, South Africa, and various states in the US—Arizona, Minnesota, Montana, New Mexico, Oklahoma, South Dakota and Wisconsin. Some bytownite crystals are shown in figure 12.27.

Choosing an Appraiser

If you were buying a classic car, you wouldn't go to the seller's mechanic to have the car checked. Hopefully, you'd take it to your own. Likewise, when you're buying expensive jewelry, you shouldn't just rely on documents provided by the seller. You should have it evaluated by an appraiser who is an unbiased third party and who has your interests in mind. Appraisals paid for by sellers are not independent appraisals.

You should get an independent jewelry appraisal:

♦ To verify the identity and quality of the gems and metals used.

♦ To get additional information about treatments, origin, and quality that the seller may not have known.

♦ To have a written third-party document that will be recognized by insurance companies. Many insurance companies do not recognize appraisals provided by the seller.

♦ To determine if you paid a fair price. It's best to consult with a professional appraiser who doesn't sell jewelry. Competing retail jewelers may downgrade and under-appraise the merchandise to get you to return the item so they can earn your trust and sell you something else at a later date. Conversely, sellers may have a tendency to give inflated appraisals. This gives them a psychological advantage and may cause you to base your decision on the deep discount they are supposedly giving you. In reality, however, the stone is worth no more than the same price you would pay somewhere else. Inflated appraisals may sound like a good idea, but they can result in unnecessarily high insurance premiums. For most insurance policies in the United States, the insurance company has the option of replacing your merchandise or paying you cash for the amount it would cost them to replace it, whichever is lower; don't expect to get cash for the value listed on an inflated appraisal.

However, you don't want an undervalued appraisal either. Obtain a legitimate appraisal from a qualified independent appraiser and avoid paying higher premiums than necessary to the insurance company. To be qualified, the appraiser must have experience in valuing the types of items and gems you want appraised.

The purpose of most appraisals is to obtain insurance coverage and to substantiate claims in the event of loss or theft. An insurance appraisal states the value of replacing a piece; it doesn't establish what you might gain in selling the piece. It must contain a thorough description of the value-making features of the jewelry in order to ensure it will be replaced with a piece of equivalent quality in case of a claim. American insurance companies seldom pay cash for a piece; they usually just buy a replacement piece at a wholesale price.

The type of appraisal that gives you the immediate cash value of your jewelry is called a liquidation appraisal. If you're only interested in a verbal estimate of how much you can sell a piece for, you can usually find that out for free. Just go to some jewelers or dealers that buy jewelry for a living and ask them what they'll pay for the piece. But be aware that the price they offer you can be lower than what you might obtain in a more competitive active market such as an auction. Independent appraisers do not offer to buy or sell your items. They have no financial investment other than fee for service.

How to Find a Qualified Independent Appraiser

Some ways to find appraisers are:

◆ Get recommendations from friends and jewelers

◆ Look through the list of independent appraisers at:

   www.reneenewman.com/appraisers.htm

◆ Write, fax or e-mail an appraisal organization and ask for the names of qualified members in your area. Listed below and on the next page are some organizations that will give you appraisers' names either verbally or on their websites.

In the USA and Canada

American Society of Appraisers (ASA)
555 Herndon Parkway, Suite 125, Herndon, VA 20170
Phone (703) 478-2228 Fax (703) 742-8471
www.appraisers.org

International Society of Appraisers (ISA)
737 North Michigan Ave, Suite 2100, Chicago, Il 60611
Phone (312) 981-6778, www.isa-appraisers.org

National Association of Jewelry Appraisers (NAJA)
P.O. Box 18, Rego Park, New York 11374-0018
Phone (718) 896-1536, www.NAJAappraisers.org

Canada

Canadian Jeweller's Institute, Phone (416) 368-7616 ext 223
27 Queen St. East Toronto, Ontario M5C 2M6 Canada
www.canadianjewellers.com/html/aapmemberlist.htm

United Kingdom and Irish Republic

The National Association of Goldsmiths' Institute of Registered Valuers
78a Luke Street, London EC2A 4XG Phone 44 020 7613 4445
www.jewelleryvaluers.org

Australia

NCJV Inc. (National Council of Jewelry Valuers)
Sydney, New South Wales, Australia, www.ncjv.com.au
Phone 02 9232 6599 Fax 02 9232 6399 Email: info@ncjv.com.au

NCJV Inc. (Queensland)
Grange, Queensland, Australia
Phone/Fax 07 3857 4377 Email: qld@ncjv.com.au

NCJV Inc. (South Australia Division)
Henley Beach, South Australia, Australia
Phone 08 8234 2505 Fax 08 8125 5822 Email: sa@ncjv.com.au

NCJV Inc. (Tasmania Division)
Hobart, Tasmania, Australia
Phone 03 6234 2426 Fax 03 6231 5366 Email: tas@ncjv.com.au

NCJV Inc., (Victoria Division)
Melbourne VIC Australia
Phone 03 9500 9250 Fax 03 9500 2904 Email: vic@ncjv.com.au

NCJV Inc., Western Australia, Australia
Perth WA Australia
Phone 08 9409 2009 Fax 08 9364 5504 Email: wa@ncjv.com.au

After you find the names of some appraisers, you'll need to interview them to find out if they're qualified to appraise your jewelry. When interviewing an appraiser you should ask:

♦ What are your qualifications?
♦ How much do you charge?
♦ What does your appraisal fee include?
♦ Have you ever appraised this type of item?

Qualifications to Look For

To appraise gems, you need to know how to identify gems and gem treatments. Competent professional appraisers should have one of the following gemological diplomas to prove they've gained the required education needed to identify gemstones.

◆ **AG (CIG)**, Accredited Gemmologist. Awarded by the Canadian Institute of Gemmology

◆ **FCGmA**, Fellow of the Canadian Gemmological Association

◆ **FGA**, Fellow of the Gemmological Association of Great Britain

◆ **FGAA**, Fellow of the Gemmological Association of Australia

◆ **FGG,** Fellow of the German Gemmological Association

◆ **GG**, Graduate Gemologist. Awarded by the Gemological Institute of America

◆ A gemologist diploma from another school or association, equivalent in stature to those listed above.

Although the gemologist diplomas listed above are important, they don't in themselves qualify people to be appraisers. Appraisers must also be skilled in valuation theory; they must be familiar with gem prices, jewelry manufacturing costs, and the legal aspects of appraising. Appraisers must have trade experience, integrity, and the initiative to keep up with the market and new developments in valuation theory and gemology.

This means appraisers should have taken appraisal courses and performed appraisal work after getting their gemologist diplomas. Some of the titles awarded to appraisers are:

AA-CJI, Accredited Appraiser of the Canadian Jeweller's Institute. Must have a gemologist diploma, a gem lab or access to a lab, three year's Canadian trade experience, must complete an appraisal course and pass a written and practical exam.

ASA, Accredited Senior Appraiser of ASA (the American Society of Appraisers). Must pass an ethics and appraisal exam, submit sample appraisals for peer review, be an accredited member of ASA and have a minimum of five years of full-time appraisal experience.

CAPP, Certified Appraiser of Personal Property. This is the highest designation offered by the International Society of Appraisers. To receive it, one must attend their appraisal courses, pass the exams, and have a gemological diploma and trade experience.

CGA, Certified Gemologist Appraiser. This is awarded by the American Gem Society to certified gemologists that pass their written and practical appraisal exam. Trade experience is a prerequisite.

CMA, Certified Master Appraiser. This is the highest award offered by NAJA (the National Association of Jewelry Appraisers). To receive it, one must have at least seven years of appraisal experience, take the NAJA appraisal studies course, pass a comprehensive theory and practical appraisal examination, and have a NAJA or AGA Certified Gem Laboratory.

CSM, Certified Senior Member of NAJA. Must have a graduate gemologist diploma, at least five years of trade and appraisal experience, at least 14 days of appraisal training and must pass the Senior Certified Member' appraisal exam.

MGA, Master Gemologist Appraiser. This is the highest level offered by the American Society of Appraisers. To receive it, a person must complete the MGA course, pass the MGA tests and have a gemologist diploma, an accredited ASA gem lab, and at least three to five years appraisal experience.

ICGA, Independent Certified Gemologist Appraiser. A designation awarded by the American Gem Society to Certified Gemologist Appraisers who also complete the three Advanced Personal Property Appraisal courses, pass the written and practical appraisal exam, refrain from buying and selling and pass an annual re-certification exam along with required documentation of continuing education in gemological and appraisal related areas.

ISA, International Society of Appraisers Accredited Member. Must pass an ethics and appraisal exam, submit sample appraisals for peer review, and have two years of full-time appraisal experience and a college degree or equivalent.

Sr. Mbr. NAJA, Must have a minimum of five years' full-time appraisal experience, accumulate a total of nineteen (19) points in education, and have fulfilled all requirements for NAJA Member status.

Besides telling you about their educational background and titles, appraisers should also discuss their experience and the type of jewelry and gems they usually appraise.

Appraisal Fees

As a consumer, you have the right to know in advance the approximate cost of an appraisal. Professional appraisers should at least be able to tell you their hourly fee and/or their minimum charge if they have one. Some will tell you a flat or approximate appraisal charge for the piece when you describe it to them over the phone. However, in fairness to the appraiser, they are entitled to change their estimate upon seeing the piece if you have played down certain areas of difficulty or have not described it fully. Appraisers have the right to refuse any item if it has a suspicious origin.

Some sellers will offer to appraise your jewelry free of charge, even if you haven't bought it from them. This is a sign that either they want to buy the jewelry from you or else they want to lure you into their store to sell you some of their merchandise. Professionals charge for their services, whether they be lawyers, doctors, accountants or appraisers.

Appraisal fees are charged in a variety of ways. Some are listed below:

◆ A flat fee per item, sometimes a lower fee for each additional piece brought in at the same time

◆ An hourly rate (often combined with a minimum fee)

◆ A rate fully or partly based on the gemstone type

◆ A rate based on the type of report you're seeking, based on the degree of work required

◆ A percentage rate of the appraised value of your jewelry. The higher the value, the more money the appraiser earns. If you want an appraisal that is as objective as possible, avoid appraisers with this type of fee structure. It's an an unethical practice if the appraiser is a member of any of the associations listed previously. The Internal Revenue Service doesn't recognize appraisals done by people who charge percentage fees. Canada doesn't accept them either.

What Does the Insurance Appraisal Include?

The key service the appraiser will provide to you is an accurate, detailed, word picture of the item you're having appraised. The structure of the resulting report will tell you something about the quality of the appraiser's work, and it will help you to better compare appraisal fees. It's understandable that a five-page report with a photo will cost more than one with only a two-sentence description and an appraised value, and you should avoid the latter type. Items that professional independent appraisers normally include with their reports are:

◆ A cleaning and inspection of the piece

◆ The identity of the stone(s) and metal(s)

◆ The measurements and estimated weights of the stones. (If you can show appraisers the exact weight of the stones on the receipt, this will help them give you a more accurate appraisal. Therefore, when buying jewelry, ask stores to write on the receipt any stone weights listed on the sales tags. A sales receipt is the only consumer protection that the buyer has.)

◆ Relevant treatment information

◆ A test of the fineness of the metals

◆ Approximate weight, measurements and description of the mounting

◆ The name(s) of the manufacturers or designers of the piece when this is known. A check must be done for fakes and fake marks.

♦ A description of the color, clarity, transparency, shape, cutting style, and cut quality of the stones. The grading and color reference system used should also be indicated. Appraisers use different color communication systems to denote color. Four of the best known are GemDialogue, Munsell, GIA GemSet, and GemESquare (or GemEPro).

♦ A photograph

♦ Definitions or explanations of the terminology used on the report

♦ A biographical sketch of the appraiser's credentials

Besides knowing what appraisers' fees include, you should know what their appraisals look like. Have them show you a sample, and check it for thoroughness and professionalism.

Jewelry appraising is an art and a science. There's a lot more to it than simply placing a dollar value on a stone or jewelry piece. If your jewelry has a great deal of monetary value, it's important that you have a detailed, accurate appraisal of it. Take as much care in selecting your appraiser as you did with your jewelry.

Bibliography

Books & Booklets

Ahrens, Joan & Malloy, Ruth. *Hong Kong Gems & Jewelry*. Hong Kong: Delta Dragon, 1986.

Anderson, B. W. *Gem Testing*. Verplanck, NY: Emerson Books, 1985.

Arem, Joel. *Color Encyclopedia of Gemstones*. New York: Chapman & Hall, 1987.

Barnson, Donna. *Ammolite 2.*Winnipeg, 2000.

Bauer, Jaroslav & Bouska, Vladimir. *Pierres Precieuses et Pierres Fines*. Paris: Bordas, 1985.

Bauer, Dr. Max. *Precious Stones Volume II*. New York: Dover Publications: 1968, English translation first published in 1904.

Bowersox, Gary & Chamberlin, Bonita. *Gemstone of Afghanistan*. Tucson: GeoScience Press, 1995.

Butler, Gail, *Crystal & Gemstone Divination*. Baldwin Park, CA: Gem Guides Book Co. 2008.

Ciprani, Curzio & Borelli, Alessandro. Simon & Schuster's Guide to Gems and Precious Stones. New York: Simon and Schuster, 1986.

Collings, Michael R. *GemLore Second Edition*. Marland: Wildside Press, 2009.

Crowe, Judith. *The Jeweler's Directory of Gemstones*. Buffalo, NY: Firefly Books, 2006.

Eason, Cassandra. *The Illustrated Directory of Healing Crystals*. London: Collins & Brown, 2004.

Federman, David & Hammid, Tino. *Consumer Guide to Colored Gemstones*. Shawnee Mission, Modern Jeweler, 1989.

Gemological Institute of America. *Gem Reference Guide*. Santa Monica, CA: GIA, 1988.

Grande, Lance, & Augustyn, Allison. *Gems & Gemstones*. Chicago: Univ. of Chicago Press, 2009.

Gubelin, Eduard J. The Color Treasury of Gemstones. New York: Thomas Y. Crowell, 1984.

Gubelin, Eduard J. & Koivula, John I. *Photoatlas of Inclusions in Gemstones, Volume 2*. Basel: Opinio Publishers, 2005.

Gubelin, Eduard J. & Koivula, John I. *Photoatlas of Inclusions in Gemstones*. Zurich: ABC Edition, 1986.

Hall, Cally. *Eyewitness Handbooks, Gemstones*. London: Dorling Kindersley, 1994.

Hall, Judy, *Crystal Bible*. Cincinnatti: Walking Stick Press, 2004.

Hall, Judy. *Illustrated Guide to Crystals*. New York: Sterling, 2000.

Hodgkinson, Alan. *Visual Optics, Diamond and Gem Identification Without Instruments*. Northbrook, IL: Gemworld International, Inc., 1995.

HRD, *Gemmology Basic Course,* Antwerp, HRD, 2005.

Jewelers of America. *The Gemstone Enhancement Manual*. New York: Jewelers of America, 2005.

Keller, Peter. *Gemstones of East Africa*. Phoenix: Geoscience Press Inc., 1992.

Kunz, George Frederick. *The Curious Lore of Precious Stones*. New York: Bell, 1989.
Kunz, George Frederick. *Gems & Precious Stones of North America*. New York: Dover, 1968.

Liddicoat, Richard T. *Handbook of Gem Identification*. Santa Monica, CA: GIA, 1989.

Matlins, Antoinette L. & Bonanno, A. *Gem Identification Made Easy*. South Woodstock, VT: Gemstone Press, 1989.
Matlins, Antoinette L. & Bonanno, A. *Jewelry & Gems: The Buying Guide*. South Woodstock: Gemstone Press, 1993.

Melody. *Love is the Earth, A Kaleidoscope of Crystals*. Wheat Ridge, CO: Earth-Love Publishing House, 1995.

Nassau, Kurt. *Gems Made by Man*. Santa Monica, CA: Gemological Institute of America, 1980.
Nassau, Kurt. *Gemstone Enhancement, Second Edition*. London: Butterworths, 1994.

Newman, Renée. *Diamond Handbook*. Los Angeles: Intl. Jewelry Publications, 2008.
Newman, Renée. *Emerald & Tanzanite Buying Guide,*. Los Angeles: Intl. Jewelry Publ., 1996.
Newman, Renée. *Gemstone Buying Guide*. Los Angeles: Intl. Jewelry Publications, 2008.

O'Donoghue, Michael, Joyner Louise. *Identification of Gemstones*. Oxford, Butterworth Heinemann, 2003.
O'Donoghue, Michael. *Identifying Man-made Gems*. London: N.A.G. Press, 1983.
O'Donoghue, Michael. *Synthetic, Imitation & Treated Gemstones*. Oxford: Butterworth-Heinemann, 1997.

Peschek-Bohmer, Schreiber, Gisela. *Healing Crystals and Gemstones*. Munich, Koneckky & Konecky, 2003.

Pough, Frederick. *Peterson Field Guides, Rocks and Minerals*. Boston: Houghton Miffln, 1983.

Read, Peter G. *Gemmology*. Oxford: Butterworth-Heineman, 1996.

Rubin, Howard & Levine. Gail, *GemDialogue Color Tool Box*. Rego Park, NY, GemDialogue Systems, Inc., 1997.
Rubin, Howard. *Grading & Pricing with GemDialogue*. New York: GemDialogue Co., 1986.

Schumann, Walter. *Gemstones of the World*. New York: Sterling, 1997.

Simmons, Robert & N. Ahsian. *Book of Stones*. Montpelier, VT: Heaven & Earth Publishing, 2005.

Sinkankas, John. *Gem Cutting: A Lapidary's Manual*. New York: Van Nostrand Reinhold, 1962.
Sinkankas, John. *Van Nostrand's Standard Catalogue of Gems*. New York: Van Nostrand Reinhold, 1968.

Skuratowicz, Arthur & Nash, Julie. *Working with Gemstones, a Bench Jeweeler's Guide*. Providence: MJSA/AJM Press, 2005.

Sofianides, Anna & Harlow, George. Gems & Crystals from the American Museum of Natural History. New York: Simon & Shuster, 1990.

Suwa, Yasukazu. *Gemstones Quality & Value (English Edition)*. GIA and Suwa & Son, Inc., 1994.

Thomas, Arthur. *The Gemstones Handbook*. UK: New Holland Publishers, 2008.

Webster, Robert. *Gemmologists' Compendium*. New York: Van Nostrand Reinhold, 1979.
Webster, Robert. *Practical Gemmology*. Ipswich, Suffolk: N. A. G. Press, 1976.

White, John S. *The Smithsonian Treasury Minerals and Gems*. Washington D.C.: Smithsonian Institution Press, 1991.

Wise, Richard. *Secrets of the Gem Trade*. Lenox, MA: Brunswick House Press, 2003.

Zancanella, Valerio. *Tanzanite*. Italy: Naturalis Historia. 2004.

Periodicals

Auction Market Resource for Gems & Jewelry. P. O. Box 7683 Rego Park, NY, 11374.

Australian Gemmologist. Brisbane: Gemmological Association of Australia

Canadian Gemmologist. Toronto: Canadian Gemmological Association.

Colored Stone. Malverne, PA: Colored Stone.

Gem & Jewellery News. London. Gemmological Association and Gem Testing Laboratory of Great Britain.

Gems and Gemology. Santa Monica, CA: Gemological Institute of America.

The GemGuide. Glenview, IL: Gemworld International, Inc.

InColor: New York, ICA (International Colored Gemstone Association)

Jewellery Business. Richmond Hill, ON, Kenilworth Media, Inc.

Jewelers Circular Keystone. Radnor, PA: Chilton Publishing Co.

JQ Magazine. San Francisco, GQ publishing..

Jewelry News Asia. Hong Kong, CMP Asia Ltd.

Jewellery Review. Hong Kong, Brilliant Art Group.

Journal of Gemmology, London: Gemmological Association and Gem Testing Laboratory of Great Britain.

Lapidary Journal Jewelry Artist. Interweave Press.

Michelsen Gemstone Index. Port Angeles, WA.

Mineralogical Record. Tucson, AZ: Mineralogical Record, Inc.

Modern Jeweler. Melville, NY: Cygnus Publishing Inc.

National Jeweler. New York: National Business Media.

Professional Jeweler. Philadelphia: Bond Communications.

Palmieri's Auction/FMV Monitor. New York, NY: GCAL

Southern Jewelry News. Greensboro, NC., *Southern Jewelry News.*

Miscellaneous: Courses, Notes, and Leaflets

Beesley, C. R., *AGL Training Manual*

Gemological Institute of America Appraisal Seminar Handbook.

Gemological Institute of America Gem Identification Course.

Gemological Institute of America Gem Identification Lab Manual

Gemological Institute of America Colored Stone Grading Course.

Gemological Institute of America Colored Stone Grading Course Charts.

Gemological Institute of America Colored Stones Course

Index

Order Form

TITLE	Price Each	Quantity	Total
Exotic Gems, Volume I	$19.95		
Ruby, Sapphire & Emerald Buying Guide	$19.95		
Gemstone Buying Guide	$19.95		
Diamond Handbook	$19.95		
Pearl Buying Guide	$19.95		
Jewelry Handbook	$19.95		
Diamond Ring Buying Guide	$18.95		
Gem & Jewelry Pocket Guide	$11.95		
Osteoporosis Prevention	$15.95		
Book Total			
SALES TAX for California residents only **(book total x $.0825)**			
SHIPPING: USA: first book $3.00, each additional copy $2.00 Canada & Mexico - airmail: first book $10.00, ea. addl. $5.00 All other foreign countries - airmail: first book $13.00, ea. addl. $7.00			
TOTAL AMOUNT with tax (if applicable) and shipping (Pay foreign orders with an international money order or a check drawn on a U.S. bank.) **TOTAL**			

Available at major book stores or by mail.

Mail check or money order in U.S. funds

To: International Jewelry Publications
P.O. Box 13384
Los Angeles, CA 90013-0384 USA

Ship to:

Name_____

Address_____

City_____ State or Province_____

Postal or Zip Code_____ Country _____

Other Books by RENÉE NEWMAN
Graduate Gemologist (GIA)

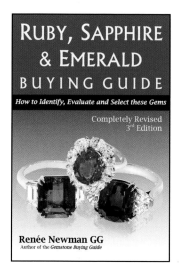

RUBY, SAPPHIRE
& EMERALD
BUYING GUIDE

How to Identify, Evaluate and Select these Gems

Completely Revised
3rd Edition

Renée Newman GG
Author of the *Gemstone Buying Guide*

Ruby, Sapphire & Emerald Buying Guide
How to Identify, Evaluate & Select these Gems

An advanced, full-color guide to identifying and evaluating rubies, sapphires and emeralds including information on treatments, grading systems, geographic sources, lab reports, appraisals, and gem care. This 3rd edition has 173 new photos and two new chapters on geographic sources and appraisals versus lab reports. It updates gem professionals on recent treatments, jewelry styles, grading systems and geographic sources of rubies, sapphires and emeralds. Tips on detecting imitations and synthetic stones are also presented.

"**Enjoyable reading . . . profusely illustrated with color photographs** showing not only the beauty of finished jewelry but close-ups and magnification of details such as finish, flaws and fakes . . . Sophisticated enough for professionals to use . . . highly recommended . . . **Newman's guides are the ones to take along when shopping**." *Library Journal*

"**Solid, informative and comprehensive** . . . dissects each aspect of ruby and sapphire value in detail . . . a wealth of grading information . . . a definite thumbs-up!"
C. R. Beesley, President, American Gemological Laboratories, *JCK Magazine*

"**A useful resource for both the experienced gemologist as well as the serious collector** . . . The book simplifies terms and explains concepts like cut, color treatments and lab reports clearly. The photographs, particularly in the sections of judging color, treatments, and clarity, are clear and true to life. All of the charts are clear and easily found and the book is well organized for quick reference. It is a handy, well organized and factually correct compilation of information with photographs that one will find themselves referencing on a regular basis."
Kindra Lovejoy, GG, *The Jewelry Appraiser*

"**The best produced book on gemstones I have yet seen in this price range** (how is it done?). This is the book for anyone who buys, sells or studies gemstones. This style of book (and similar ones by the same author) is the only one I know which introduces actual trade conditions and successfully combines a good deal of gemmology with them . . . **Buy it, read it, keep it**."
Michael O'Donoghue, *Journal of Gemmology*

187 pages, 280 photos, 267 in color, 6" by 9", US$19.95, ISBN 978-0929975412

Available at major bookstores and jewelry supply stores

For more information, see **www.reneenewman.com**

Other Books by RENÉE NEWMAN

Graduate Gemologist (GIA)

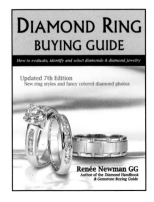

Diamond Ring Buying Guide

How to Evaluate, Identify and Select
Diamonds & Diamond Jewelry

"**An entire course on judging diamonds in 156 pages of well-organized information**. The photos are excellent . . . Clear and concise, it serves as a check-list for the purchase and mounting of a diamond . . . another fine update in a series of books that are useful to both the jewelry industry and consumers." *Gems & Gemology*

"**A wealth of information** . . . delves into the intricacies of shape, carat weight, color, clarity, setting style, and cut—happily avoiding all industry jargon and keeping explanations streamlined enough so even the first-time diamond buyer can confidently choose a gem." *Booklist*

"Succinctly written in a step-by-step, outlined format with plenty of photographs to illustrate the salient points; it could help keep a lot of people out of trouble. Essentially, it is a **fact-filled text devoid of a lot of technical mumbo-jumbo.** This is a definite thumbs up!"

C. R. Beesley, President, American Gemological Laboratories

156 pages, 274 color & b/w photos, 7" X 9", ISBN 978-0-929975-40-5, US$18.95

Gem & Jewelry Pocket Guide

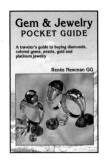

Small enough to use while shopping locally or abroad

"**Brilliantly planned, painstakingly researched, and beautifully produced** . . . this handy little book comes closer to covering all of the important bases than any similar guides have managed to do. From good descriptions of the most popular gem materials (plus gold and platinum), to jewelry craftsmanship, treatments, gem sources, appraisals, documentation, and even information about U.S. customs for foreign travelers—it is all here. I heartily endorse this wonderful pocket guide."

John S. White, former Curator of Gems & Minerals at the Smithsonian
Lapidary Journal

"**Short guides don't come better than this**. . . . As always with this author, the presentation is immaculate and each opening displays high-class pictures of gemstones and jewellery." *Journal of Gemmology*

156 pages, 108 color photos, 4½" by 7", ISBN 978-0929975-30-6, US$11.95

Available at major bookstores and jewelry supply stores

For more information, see **www.reneenewman.com**

Pearl Buying Guide

How to Evaluate, Identify, Select and Care for Pearls & Pearl Jewelry

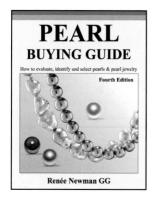

"**Copious color photographs** . . . explains how to appraise and distinguish among all varieties of pearls . . . takes potential buyers and collectors through the ins and outs of the pearl world." *Publisher's Weekly*

"**An indispensable guide** to judging [pearl] characteristics, distinguishing genuine from imitation, and making wise choices . . . useful to all types of readers, from the professional jeweler to the average patron . . . **highly recommended.**" *Library Journal*

"A **well written, beautifully illustrated** book designed to help retail customers, jewelry designers, and store buyers make informed buying decisions about the various types of pearls and pearl jewelry. The photos are abundant and well chosen, and the use of a coated stock contributes to the exceptional quality of the reproduction. Consumers also will find this book a source of accurate and easy-to-understand information about a topic that has become increasingly complex."

Gems & Gemology

154 pages, 208 color & b/w photos, 6" by 9", ISBN 978-0929975-44-3, US$19.95

Jewelry Handbook

How to Select, Wear & Care for Jewelry

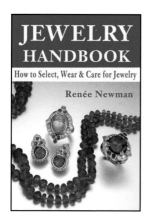

The *Jewelry Handbook* is like a Jewelry 101 course on the fundamentals of jewelry metals, settings, finishes, necklaces, chains, clasps, bracelets, rings, earrings, brooches, pins, clips, manufacturing methods and jewelry selection and care. It outlines the benefits and drawbacks of the various setting styles, mountings, chains, and metals such as gold, silver, platinum, palladium, titanium, stainless steel and tungsten. It also provides information and color photos on gemstones, birthstones, and fineness marks and helps you select versatile, durable jewelry that flatters your features.

"A **great introduction to jewellery** and should be required reading for all in the industry." Dr. Jack Ogden, CEO Gem-A (British Gemmological Association)

"A **user-friendly, beautifully illustrated guide,** allowing for quick reference to specific topics." *The Jewelry Appraiser*

"**Valuable advice for consumers and the trade**, specifically those in retail sales and perhaps even more for jewelry appraisers . . . An easy read and easy to find valuable lists and details." Richard Drucker GG, *Gem Market News*

177 pages, 297 color & 47 b/w photos, 6" x 9", ISBN 978-0-929975-38-2, $19.95 US

Other Books by RENÉE NEWMAN

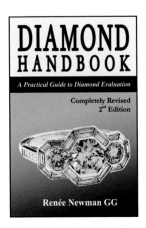

Diamond Handbook
A Practical Guide to Diamond Evaluation

Updates professionals on new developments in the diamond industry and provides advanced information on diamond grading, treatments, synthetic diamonds, fluorescence, and fancy colored diamonds. It also covers topics not in the *Diamond Ring Buying Guide* such as diamond grading reports, light performance, branded diamonds, diamond recutting, and antique diamond cuts and jewelry.

"Impressively comprehensive. . . . a **practical, well-organized and concisely written** volume, packed with valuable information. The *Diamond Handbook* is destined to become an indispensable reference for the consumer and trade professional alike."
Canadian Gemmologist

"The text covers everything the buyer needs to know, with useful comments on lighting and first-class images. No other text in current circulation discusses recutting and its possible effects . . . **This is a must for anyone buying, testing or valuing a polished diamond and for students in many fields.**" *Journal of Gemmology*

186 pages, 320 photos (most in color), 6" x 9", ISBN 978-0-929975-39-9, $19.95

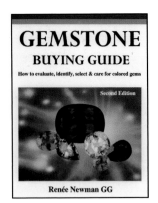

Gemstone Buying Guide
How to Evaluate, Identify and Select
Colored Gems

"Praiseworthy, a beautiful gem-pictorial reference and a help to everyone in viewing colored stones as a gemologist or gem dealer would. . . . One of the finest collections of gem photographs I've ever seen . . . If you see the book, you will probably purchase it on the spot."
Anglic Gemcutter

"A quality Buying Guide that is recommended for purchase to consumers, gemmologists and students of gemmology—irrespective of their standard of knowledge of gemmology. The information is comprehensive, factual, and well presented. Particularly noteworthy in this book are the quality colour photographs that have been carefully chosen to illustrate the text." *Australian Gemmologist*

"Beautifully produced. . . . With colour on almost every opening few could resist this book whether or not they were in the gem and jewellery trade."
Journal of Gemmology

156 pages, 281 color photos, 7" X 9", ISBN 978-0929975-34-4, US$19.95

Osteoporosis Prevention

" . . . a complete, practical, and easy-to-read reference for osteoporosis prevention . . . As the founding president of the Taiwan Osteoporosis Association, I am delighted to recommend this book to you."

Dr. Ko-En Huang, Founding President of TOA

"The author, Renée Newman has abundant experience in translating technical terms into everyday English. She writes this book about osteoporosis prevention from a patient's perspective. These two elements contribute to an easy-to-read and understandable book for the public. To the medical professions, this is also a very valuable reference."

Dr. Chyi-Her Lin, Dean of Medical College, Natl Cheng Kung Univ / Taiwan

"I was impressed with the comprehensive nature of *Osteoporosis Prevention* and its use of scientific sources . . . . The fact that the author has struggled with bone loss and can talk from personal experience makes the book more interesting and easy to read. Another good feature is that the book has informative illustrations and tables, which help clarify important points. I congratulate the author for writing a sound and thorough guide to osteoporosis prevention." Ronald Lawrence, MD, PhD

Co-chair of the first Symposium on Osteoporosis of the National Institute on Aging

" . . . clarifies the inaccurate concepts from the Internet. It contains abundant information and really deserves my recommendation."

Dr. Yung-Kuei Soong, The 6th President of Taiwanese Osteoporosis Association

"The book is written from a patient's experience and her secrets to bone care. This book is so interesting that I finished reading it the following day . . . The author translates all the technical terms into everyday English which makes this book so easy to read and understand."

Dr. Sheng-Mou Hou, Ex-minister, Dept. of Health / Taiwan

"A competent and thoroughly 'reader friendly' approach to preventing osteoporosis. Inclusive of information on how to: help prevent osteoporosis and broken bones; get enough calcium and other bone nutrients from food; make exercise safe and fun; retain a youthful posture; select a bone density center; get maximum benefit from your bone density exam; understand bone density reports; help seniors maintain their muscles and their bones; and how to be a savvy patient. *Osteoporosis Prevention* should be a part of every community health center and public library Health & Medicine reference collection . . ."

Midwest Book Review

"With great interest, I have read Renée Newman's *Osteoporosis Prevention* which provides complete and practical information about osteoporosis from a patient's perspective. . . . a must-read reference for osteoporosis prevention."

Dr. Tzay-Shing Yang, 3rd President of TOA, President of Taiwan Menopause Care Society

You can get free information about osteoporosis prevention, bone density testing and reports at: **www.avoidboneloss.com**

176 pages, 6" X 9", US $15.95, ISBN 978-0929975-37-5

Order Form

TITLE	Price Each	Quantity	Total
Exotic Gems, Volume I	$19.95		
Ruby, Sapphire & Emerald Buying Guide	$19.95		
Gemstone Buying Guide	$19.95		
Diamond Handbook	$19.95		
Pearl Buying Guide	$19.95		
Jewelry Handbook	$19.95		
Diamond Ring Buying Guide	$18.95		
Gem & Jewelry Pocket Guide	$11.95		
Osteoporosis Prevention	$15.95		
		Book Total	
SALES TAX for California residents only	**(book total x $.0825)**		
SHIPPING: USA: first book $3.00, each additional copy $2.00 Canada & Mexico - airmail: first book $10.00, ea. addl. $5.00 All other foreign countries - airmail: first book $13.00, ea. addl. $7.00			
TOTAL AMOUNT with tax (if applicable) and shipping (Pay foreign orders with an international money order or a check drawn on a U.S. bank.)		**TOTAL**	

Available at major book stores or by mail.

Mail check or money order in U.S. funds

To: International Jewelry Publications
P.O. Box 13384
Los Angeles, CA 90013-0384 USA

Ship to:

Name_____

Address_____

City_____ State or Province_____

Postal or Zip Code_____ Country _____